THE LONG EMANCIPATION

RINALDO WALCOTT

MOVING

THE LONG

TOWARD

EMANCIPATION

BLACK FREEDOM

Duke University Press   *Durham and London*   2021

Printed in the United States of America on acid-free paper ∞
Designed by Courtney Leigh Richardson and typeset in Minion Pro
and Trade Gothic by Copperline Book Services

Library of Congress Cataloging-in-Publication Data
Names: Walcott, Rinaldo, [date] author.
Title: The long emancipation : moving toward black freedom /
Rinaldo Walcott.
Description: Durham : Duke University Press, 2021. | Includes
bibliographical references and index.
Identifiers: LCCN 2020027617 (print)
LCCN 2020027618 (ebook)
ISBN 9781478011910 (hardcover)
ISBN 9781478014058 (paperback)
ISBN 9781478021360 (ebook)
Subjects: LCSH: Blacks—United States—Social conditions. |
Marginality, Social—United States—History. | Racism—United
States. | Blacks—Caribbean Area—Social conditions. | Marginality,
Social—Caribbean Area. | Racism—Caribbean Area.
Classification: LCC E185.86 .W3345 2021 (print) |
LCC E185.86 (ebook) | DDC 973/.0496073—dc23
LC record available at https://lccn.loc.gov/2020027617
LC ebook record available at https://lccn.loc.gov/2020027618

Cover art: *A Single Section: The Journey #3*, 2016, acrylic on canvas,
60 × 60 in. © Torkwase Dyson. Courtesy of the artist.

For Abdi Osman WHO IS EVERYTHING.

CONTENTS

ACKNOWLEDGMENTS ix

1 MOVING TOWARD BLACK FREEDOM 1
2 BLACK LIFE-FORMS 9
3 DEATH AND FREEDOM 11
4 BLACK DEATH 15
5 PLANTATION ZONES 19
6 DIASPORA STUDIES 23
7 THE ATLANTIC REGION AND 1492 27
8 NEW STATES OF BEING 33
9 THE LONG EMANCIPATION 35
10 CATASTROPHE, WAKE, HAUNTOLOGY 43
11 BODIES OF WATER 47
12 SLAVE SHIP LOGICS/LOGISTICS 51
13 PROBLEM OF THE HUMAN,
   OR THE VOID OF RELATIONALITY 55
14 NO HAPPY STORY 59
15 I REALLY WANT TO HOPE 65
16 FUNK: A BLACK NOTE ON THE HUMAN 69
17 NEWNESS 75
18 TOWARD A SAGGIN' PANTS ETHICS 81
19 BLACK MEN, STYLE, AND FASHION 87
20 NO FUTURE 91
21 (FUTURE) BLACK STUDIES 99
22 THE LONG EMANCIPATION REVISITED 105

NOTES 111
BIBLIOGRAPHY 119
INDEX 125

ACKNOWLEDGMENTS

This essay exists because of persistence. All of it faults, limitations, mistakes, and missed opportunities can be credited to me. I begin these acknowledgments in the negative because a short and small book about freedom is a risk. But freedom, or the desire for it, especially by Black people, is a risk too. The idea for this essay began when Katherine McKittrick and *Antipode: A Radical Journal of Geography* invited me to give the Antipode lecture at the American Geographers Association meeting in 2014 in Tampa, Florida. I thank them very much for the opportunity that made this essay thinkable and possible. The invitation sparked in me the idea that I might have something to say about freedom, an idea that has stayed with me in a powerful way. From that lecture the idea of the long emancipation as both a phrase and a concept was further cemented when the graduate students of the Department of English at McGill University invited me to give a keynote at their conference in 2015. It was between those two invitations that the idea of the long emancipation was confirmed for me as something worth pursuing and sharing with others.

Most powerfully, the problem of freedom for Black people impressed itself on me in the era of the Obama presidency and the spectacularization of Black death across North America and beyond. For almost one full day and mostly into the night, Christina Sharpe and I DMed each other on Twitter after images of Mike Brown lying dead and uncovered in the streets of Ferguson appeared online and protests broke out there. The Movement for Black Lives was (re)ignited with the murder of Trayvon Martin, but Mike Brown's death crystallized something about Black people and freedom that remains difficult to articulate, even after writing the words here. I profusely thank Christina for everything she has done to make this essay a reality. It has come to this stage primarily because of her; she refused to let me abandon it.

Black Lives Matter is a central and unnamed figure in this work. The Movement for Black Lives and Black Lives Matter – Toronto and the larger organization have made me think very hard about what I have tried to articulate in these pages. Contemporary Black activist politics is what made it necessary for me to write these words. I thank Idil Abdillahi for insisting that I risk my ideas in activist circles and for her reading of a draft of this essay and also insisting that I see it through into publication.

Additional thanks to Andenye Chablit-Clarke; editors Heather Sangster and Jacqui Shine, who worked on this text in different ways; and the anonymous reviewers. To my friends and colleagues who have lived with me talking about the ideas in this work, but never seeing the final manuscript, you know who you are. I thank you for believing it was an actual thing that I was actually trying to make possible.

I also wish to thank Sabine Broeck, who invited me to Bremen University and conferences where some of these ideas were first presented. To Susan Arndt and Mariam Popal, who arranged a fellowship at Bayreuth University, where a bulk of the initial writing occurred, I thank you immensely for your generosity and intellectual community. This essay is so much richer because of your commitments to Black/African intellectual life and your willingness to be profoundly challenged by Black people who speak back. In Germany, Nadja Ofuatey-Alazard and Phillipa Ebene made Bayreuth, Munich, and Berlin wonderful Black diasporic spaces, and I am blessed to know you both; you remind me constantly of how intimately Africa remains tied to its diaspora.

At the very moment that I had decided to give up on this project, my friends, interlocutors, and intellectual giants Dionne Brand and Christina Sharpe literally showed up at our house and sat with me and demanded that I attend to the revisions. There exist no words to thank them enough for their unwavering support of me and, more important, their support for what I am attempting in these pages. Insistence is grace, Dionne has written, and I experienced it as such.

The completion of this work is shrouded in loss: friends, strangers, activists. The struggle for freedom is a fierce and unrelenting one. It is one in which giving up is simply not an option for Black people. The artists Torkwase Dyson and Paulo Nazareth have been generous in providing permission to use their important work that inspires me. Generally speaking, Black and nonwhite artists and thinkers sit at the foundation of this text. I have been inspired by them, and I am in conversation with them even when it might not appear as explicit. They have been my intellectual lifeline for more than two decades.

And then there is Ken Wissoker, the senior executive editor of Duke University Press and an intellectual and quite frankly lovely supporter of ideas and taking risks. I thank him immensely for staying with this project and also insisting it come into existence; and the staff: the folks at Duke University Press are simply the best—your patience for slow and tardy writers (and reviewers like me) is magical and worth emulating everywhere. Thank you for sticking with me and especially for sticking with this small project. The flaws remain mine nonetheless.

PARTS OF THIS BOOK were published as "The Problem of the Human: Black Ontologies and 'the Coloniality of Our Being,'" in *Postcoloniality—Decoloniality—Black Critique: Joints and Fissures*, edited by Sabine Broeck and Carsten Junker (Frankfurt: Campus Verlag, 2014), 93–106; "Freedom Now Suite: Black Feminist Turns of Voice," *Small Axe* 22, no. 3 (57) (2018): 151–59; and "Diaspora, Transnationalism, and the Decolonial Project," in *Otherwise Worlds: Against Settler Colonialism and Anti-Blackness*, edited by Tiffany Lethabo King, Jenell Navarro, and Andrea Smith (Durham, NC: Duke University Press, 2020), 343–61.

1. MOVING TOWARD BLACK FREEDOM

Time would pass, old empires would fall and new ones take their place, the relations of countries and the relations of classes had to change, before I discovered that it is not quality of goods and utility which matter, but movement: not where you are or what you have, but where you have come from, where you are going and the rate at which you are getting there.

—C. L. R. JAMES, *Beyond a Boundary* (1963)

Set the captives free.

—BOB MARLEY, "Exodus," from *Exodus* (1977)

The conditions of Black life, past and present, work against any notion that what we inhabit in the now is freedom. Postslavery and postcolony, Black people, globally, have yet to experience freedom. We remain in the time of emancipation. *Emancipation* is commonly understood as the "freeing of the slaves" in the post-Columbus world, but emancipation is a legal process and term that I will argue marks continued unfreedom, *not* the freedom it supposedly ushered in. The legal parameters of emancipation in each region were different, but in no instance did emancipation give the formerly enslaved the right simply to leave their surroundings. In the British emancipation proclamation, for example, the formerly enslaved were to serve as apprentices for up to seven years (1834–40). It was the ex-slaves' resistance to apprenticeship that led to a speeding up of emancipation. It is in the moment of accelerated legal emancipation that the contours of freedom, or a potential freedom, begin to take shape for Black people. In fact, one must note that at every moment Black peoples have sought, for themselves, to assert what freedom might mean and look like, those desires and acts toward freedom have been violently interdicted. It is this ongoing interdiction of a potential Black freedom that I have termed *the long emancipation*.

In this essay, *The Long Emancipation: Moving toward Black Freedom*, I argue that we are still in the time of emancipation and that freedom, which is extra-emancipation or beyond the logic of emancipation, is yet to come.

What, then, is freedom? What am I defining as freedom? How do I demarcate why and how Black peoples do not yet have something called freedom? I understand emancipation as always embedded in the juridical and thus as always orienting and delimiting freedom. Freedom resists guarantees of comportment. I define freedom as ways of being human in the world that exist beyond the realm of the juridical and that allow for bodily sovereignty. I argue that freedom marks an individual and a collective desire to be *in common* and *in difference* in a world that is nonhierarchical and nonviolent. It marks, as well, the social, political, and imaginative conditions that make possible multiple ways of being in the world. With the phrases *in common* and *in difference*, I am stressing that collective commonality can occur alongside individual self-actualization. In other words, the ways that human beings share common experiences of the world we inhabit do not have to erase individual wants, desires, and needs. But the time of the long emancipation continues to tie Black people to the regimen of slave and plantation logics and economies. The idea of freedom that I am attempting to articulate here is one that imagines a break with those logics.

Indeed, most definitions of freedom are circular, repeating the word *freedom* or *free*, which is then rendered in opposition to something else: in this sense, one is often freed (passive voice) from or to A or B as an expression of freedom. Black freedom is often offered only in opposition to the history of enslavement—an idea that recognizes the former (slavery) but struggles to articulate what we do not yet have a language for (something more). I suggest that, especially for Black people, the idea of freedom contains both oppositionality and the something more. By making such a claim, I am interested in examining what I call *glimpses of Black freedom*, those moments of the something more that exist inside of the dire conditions of our present Black unfreedom. To glimpse Black freedom requires that those of us who look for it reject the modes of looking and assessing freedom that blackness itself often refuses. The major ideals of modernity that constitute the normative registers of recognizing freedom do not, in fact, give us insight into the ways that Black beings make something like freedom appear. Blackness's refusals include, but are not limited to, representative democracy; the institution of policing; modes of comportment in terms of fashion, style, and attitude; reformist logics that retain the present shape of the world; nationalisms of all kinds; as well as a more generally assumed mode of human life as one of linear progression and human perfection. I suggest that the conditions of a potential Black freedom remain outside of modernity's imagining. There is a tension within the logic of modernist freedom, which assumes a linearity—that one perfects *what it means to be human* in a linear fashion. That maturation narrative is one in which, for example, first we can recognize white women as human beings, and then we can recognize white gays and lesbians as humans, and that recognition offers a kind of fulfillment of the promise of freedom. Black freedom, I argue, is much more eruptive and much more disruptive than the so-called freedoms offered up by that kind of narrative.

Black freedom, or a potential Black freedom, exposes that tension and refuses that kind of linear narrative. A potential Black freedom is more like a set of eruptions that push against and within how we have come to understand what freedom is, that push against what is often offered to us as a logic of the maturation of human life. As Saidiya Hartman has articulated so clearly in *Scenes of Subjection*, that "burdened individuality" gives the lie to the logic of liberalism's linear progressive narrative precisely because of the ways that modernist logics of freedom are deployed against Black people and how Black people themselves have largely come to imagine what freedom might be.[1] Put another way, all of our present conceptions of freedom, understood within that linear progressive narrative, actually prohibit Black subjects' access to that very same linear modernist freedom.

What, then, is the long emancipation? It is the continuation of the juridical and legislative status of Black nonbeing. The use of the term *emancipation* as a synonym for *freedom* can only continue to make sense because it is through legislative and juridical practices and regimes that Black people come into a status that is other than that of being the enslaved. In other words, this logic can only hold if freedom, as far as the Black is concerned, is legislative and conferred. What emancipation does not do is to make a sharp and necessary break with the social relations that underpin slavery. That this break has not yet happened is why we are still in the period of emancipation. We recognize this as it plays out in our present times in the ways that other modes of the legislative and the juridical come into play through social proscriptions around Black dress and movement, from baseball caps and saggin' pants to stop-and-frisk and carding to what Frank Wilderson identifies as the ongoing "ipso facto" deputization of white people.[2] These proscriptions are, in effect, the legacies of a juridical emancipated Black status that remains tied to the social relations and former conditions of enslavement.

Whether we are speaking of the time of emancipation in the British Caribbean or in the United States, the legislation passed to end chattel slavery did not allow those newly unowned peoples fully to become a part of the polities where they live. Instead, emancipation legislation held the formerly enslaved in captive relationship to their very recent past.[3] By so doing, emancipation legislation sets up a structure in which the newly emancipated are tutored, in often degrading fashion, into a new reorienting political and social polity. In that new polity, Black people are placed in a position of subordinated lives in which further resistance continues to push the boundaries of what constitutes emancipation. But I insist that Black people do experience moments of freedom that are unscripted, imaginative, and beyond our current modes of intelligibility. Each push by the formerly enslaved is an eruption of a potential Black freedom, but each push is also contained by the juridical and legislative elasticity of the logic of emancipation as partial, as incremental, as apprenticed.

In these pages, I explore the potential of Black freedom, and I point to how we might dwell in its fleeting moments. The central conceit of this work is to grapple with a desired sovereignty of Black being, a desire that Toni Morrison, in *Beloved*, puts into the mouth of Baby Suggs. Sethe, in her "rememory" of Baby Suggs, remembers it this way:

> In this here place, we flesh; flesh that weeps, laughs; flesh that dances on bare feet in grass. Love it. Love it hard. Yonder they do not love your flesh. They despise it. . . . No more do they love the skin on your back. Yonder they flay it. And O my people they do not love your hands. Those they only use, tie, bind, chop off and leave empty. Love your hands! Love them. Raise them up and kiss them. Touch others with them, pat them together, stroke them on your face 'cause they don't love that either. You got to love it, you! And no, they ain't in love with your mouth. Yonder, out there, they will see it broken and break it again. What you say out of it they will not heed. . . . What you put into it to nourish your body they will snatch away and give leavins instead. No they don't love your mouth. *You* got to love it. This is flesh I'm talking about here. Flesh that needs to be loved. Feet that need to rest and to dance; backs that need support; shoulders that need arms, strong arms I'm telling you. And O my people, out yonder, hear me, they do not love your neck unnoosed and straight. So love your neck; put a hand on it, grace it, stroke it and hold it up. And all your inside parts that they'd just as soon slop for hogs, you got to love them. The dark, dark liver—love it, love it, and the beat and beating heart, love that too. More than eyes or feet. . . . More than

your life-holding womb and your life-giving private parts, hear me now, love your heart. For this is the prize.[4]

With Baby Suggs's sermon in the Clearing, Morrison offers us an engagement with the Black body and Black personhood as sites onto which the conditions of freedom and unfreedom are projected. Reading this sermon points to that which must be undone so that Black freedom might be glimpsed globally. The reclaiming of the flesh as a body, a body loved, is a glimpse of freedom in its kinetic form where freedom meets love, and where love becomes an activating force toward a potential freedom. In this instance, freedom exists beyond the material even though it is also, and importantly, material conditions. Indeed, love, a nonmaterial condition, becomes a major context for moving toward freedom. Freedom as imminent condition — Derridean language on democracy as that which is "to come" might point us toward this — is both belated and always just ahead of us. Black freedom has been denied despite juridical emancipation, and that denial produces the conditions of a future-oriented Black expressivity — a Black freedom to come. It is my argument that Black life most clearly reveals the limits of the conditions of freedom because Black life seems to dwell in that Derridean "to come" that is always anticipatory and future-oriented. Black life points us toward what freedom might be, and ultimately is, a project yet to come.

Any serious student of Black life can but note the multiple ways in which freedom is continually interdicted and prohibited for Black subjects. And yet Black people's desires for freedom and to be free find expression in their resistances to ways of being that would deny them bodily sovereignty (through their embodiment, community formations, etc.). In this work, I think what lies between that which is prohibited and that which is gestured to can offer insights into and evidence of a freedom to come. Furthermore, Black freedom is not just freedom for Black subjects; it is a freedom that inaugurates an entirely new human experience for everyone. Black freedom, then, is not one kind of freedom that sits alongside other kinds of freedom; it is a global reorienting and radical reordering phenomenon. This is not an exceptionalist argument on behalf of Black people but an accounting of the ways that Black people's dispossession and its possible rectification would require global reordering, rethinking, and remaking; such an accounting would mean a reorientation of the planet and all modes of being human on it. With such an accounting, new registers of life would appear.

Where we see glimpses of Black freedom to come, we see it as the Black body configures and reconfigures modes of being in the world, often in the vernacular cultures of Black people's everyday and ordinary lives. The manner in which Black people "own" their bodies and the ways in which music, dance, clothing, attitude(s), posture, affect, optic, and opinion keep language and a range of practices both tied closely to the body and emanating from it allow for us to glimpse Black freedom in fleeting moments. Again, in noticing such practices, the material conditions and something beyond them are marked as central to thinking what freedom can be. I turn to several vernacular moments and practices, to think about how Black freedom and unfreedom register and the ways in which those practices are violently interdicted. When I speak of the vernacular, I mean to note all of those moments of creativity of Black beings that initially exist outside of or in response to dominant and normative institutions and modes of being. The vernacular marks Black inventiveness and Black ways of being that create Black self-conscious worlds. The vernacular is a particularly fertile site for thinking about Black freedom because the vernacular is, contradictorily and simultaneously, a sovereign site of Black expressivity and creativity and one of the most heavily policed and interdicted sites of Black life.

Black Power and the Black Arts Movement attempted to bring Black vernacular practices into existence as legitimate modes of being Black in the world for both Black people and others, and in many ways they were successful. These political and artistic moments self-consciously aestheticized what was formerly degraded and dismissed. Such practices offer contemporary critics a different way to think about the work of the Black vernacular as enacting and pointing to a potential Black freedom. Indeed, the white state's supremacist response to Black Power and the Black Arts Movement demonstrates that these attempts, or acts, of a potential freedom must too be undermined and violently interdicted — thus the genesis of the surveillance and infiltration project of the FBI's Counter Intelligence Program (COINTELPRO) and, more recently, the agency's creation of the "Black Identity Extremist" designation to apply to Black activists.

Nonetheless, Black people continue to find ways of engaging vernacular practices in which to narrate their lives to themselves — *from within and against* the proscribed conditions set by white supremacy. As Robin D. G. Kelley has long pointed out, Black men have remade the street corner as one site of communal gathering that is both labor and pleasure.[5] At the same time, a site like the corner is policed by the state and understood as in opposition to whiteness as the only proper form of comportment. Such eruptions of freedom are also policed by forms of Black respectability premised on a linear modernist notion of freedom that is (un)consciously drawn from a template for whiteness. Black women have remade hair as fashion beyond the haircut or "hairstyle," and Black women's hair remains a significant site of cultural debate, disgust, and cultural appropriation. In the midst of such approbation and disgust, and attacked with the (dubious) category of female beauty based in whiteness, Black women create lifeworlds in which their modes of speech, their "hairstyles," and even their bodily parts are replicated and desired and claimed as beautiful on others, not them.[6] Black vernacular forms, whether bodily or of another form of materiality, when appropriated are often capitalized and celebrated in service of others. All of this marks what I call the long emancipation, where one does not have full possession of one's being and where the one, in fact, who would claim ownership over you is compensated and not the one (Black) who is doing the labor.

To think these ambivalences and contradictions, this work grapples with the insights of Sylvia Wynter, that philosopher of the Americas, in "1492: A New World View," on questions of the human and the requirement that we (re)think what the human might be. In a world where Black people have been ejected from the category of the human and have struggled both to enter it and to reanimate what it might/can mean, (re)thinking the human is central to any notion of a freedom for which we do not yet have the words. Following Frantz Fanon in *Black Skin, White Masks* and Wynter in "1492: A New World View," *The Long Emancipation* is committed to the notion of a new humanism, beginning in the acknowledgment that our present conceptions of what it means to be human and a subject do not currently include Black people. Indeed, such conceptions of the human cannot contain them.[7]

It is not too much to claim that postslavery renovations of the human have continually produced a brutal outside for blackness and Black peoples globally. Black life-form(s) are a significant critique of the currently brutal realities of what it means to be human in the world. I come to this articulation of Black life-form(s) in conversation with Frantz Fanon, Sylvia Wynter, Édouard Glissant, Kamau Brathwaite, Saidiya Hartman, and Jacques Derrida, among many others.

What Wynter refers to as "the dysselected others" — that is, Black subjects — I, in turn, imagine and define as *Black life-forms*, a stark term that makes clear the stakes of the matter at hand. I use the term *Black life-forms* because Euro-American definitions and practices of the human offer Black life no conceptual or actual space within the terrain of the human. Black life-forms are forced to make the deadly zone of the Americas a residence and a site of life-making. Their presence marks the significant residuals of all that has come to constitute what we call the human, with Black life-forms standing as the human's antagonist and, therefore, its hindrance. Black life-forms remind those who lay claim to the human that modernity's claim of the perfection of human life is impossible. That claim is premised on a singular role for "the Black," that of violent death. The zone of the Americas is a zone of and for the production of Black death. My insistence on death is not to suggest that Black life does not happen, but rather that death is the means toward Black life. By this I mean that the constant urgency of living with death for Black people conditions how they understand their lives. In particular, I think of Haiti and the enormity of death that produces, nonetheless, vibrant forms of religion, dance, ritual, and art that are expressive of the deep recesses of what it means to inhabit a *livedness of being*. Indeed, the "discovery" of the Americas inaugurates a relation to Black nonhumanness that we still live in the present. I consciously use the word *discovery* here because it spectacularizes the conditions of life and death launched with the arrival of the Euro-American expansionist project. And that spectacle is crucial to how we understand genres of the human. Those genres of the human provided us with a set of racial hierarchies and relations to life and death that continue to shape Black people's experiences globally. What this means is that Black life-forms allow us to see other ways of being human and thus other possible ways of living. Black life-forms remain a significant challenge to Euro-American *partial forms of life.*

With the term *Black life-forms* I also mean to further elaborate the ways that Black people must make a claim to each genre of the human, whether that genre is LGBTQI persons, persons living with disabilities, or others. In each instance, Black people must insist "us too." The Black life-form, therefore, is an acknowledgment that we exist, we are alive, we are a site of life. But the Black life-form also seeks to call into disrepute and indict our present system of being human—a system that, as I will argue in this work, is founded on the expulsion of Black people from the definition of what it is to be human.

This work grapples with that ongoing brutality in the face of global human rights discourses that I argue cannot imagine Black people as rights-bearing subjects and therefore as subjects for freedom. Following C. L. R. James and the epigraph to the previous section, one might most starkly see the collapse of such human rights discourses when Black subjects move, as is so chillingly clear with the contemporary movement of Black people from the continent to Europe, across the Strait of Gibraltar, or the simple act of going swimming in McKinney, Texas, or in other places in the United States and Canada, where Black people are murdered for playing music too loud, for committing traffic offenses, for walking in one's own community, for suffering mental health breaks like Abdirahman Abdi in Ottawa, and on it goes. It becomes glaringly apparent that human rights discourses contract when the Black subject appears.

The death of Black selves is central to any freedom to come. It is at the point of Black death and the multiple ways in which Black people die that unfreedom most glaringly reveals itself. Put another way, because Black people die differently, it is at the moment of our deaths that the work of unfreedom reveals itself. When I say that Black people die differently, I mean that our deaths are simultaneously spectacularized and disregarded even as the actual conditions of our deaths might appear to mirror those deaths of others. For example, Black people in North America continue to die from HIV/AIDS at rates that most other North Americans do not. Even more so, however, Black people still die from what we used to call full-blown AIDS in the time that we now know as postcocktail. This is an example of how we die differently and how the time of emancipation stretches across various times and eras.

The conditions of Black life are constricted and bounded by the vicious realities of anti-Black violences. For the Black subject, freedom and death seem to have an indelible link: both work as escapes to constitute a marking of blackness that is bounded and yet demands an unboundedness toward another state of being. Both freedom and death work as escapes from the brutal realities of the present. Death ends the earthly or worldly brutal conditions. The desire for modernist freedom, a freedom that is linear and progressive, is experienced and lived as an anticipated relief from those same brutal worldly conditions. Freedom and death seem to offer an anticipated boundlessness to Black life; thus, in some Afro-Christian religions, the refrain of "in the by and by" conjoins freedom and death. Richard Iton, for example, turns to the Black love song and more generally Black popular music in his book *In Search of the Black Fantastic* to illustrate the constriction of Black heterosexuality, as a metaphor for political conditions and the excessiveness of the black fantastic (via the love song) or its aesthetic that becomes unbounded as a form of freedom.[1] In another view, Black people's potential freedom would inaugurate new ways of living not yet fully seen.

As I sit and write these words, reports of Black death continue to circulate across the globe. The deaths I mark here are deaths at the hands of state institutions such as the police and their global practices such as prisons and refugee and immigration detention camps, which produce Black life as a lesser life or as nonlife. Black women, men, and children are all subject to what some call "extrajudicial" death within and across various nation-states. Yet the problem with utilizing a category such as "extrajudicial" is that it assumes that Black life is recognizable as a life under and in the context of modernity and its orders of knowledge, juridical rules, and conditions that recognize some lives as a life. These deaths at the hands of police and other state actors and substate actors are so frequent and so numerous as to be a natural part of Black life.

Black death orients Black life in ways that produce Black life both in deeply restricted ways and as excess. The magnitude of ongoing Black death restricts and contracts how Black people experience the world, and yet Black death also requires from Black people forms of life and living that reorient and erupt and change it all for everybody. What Black folks do in the face of these death-bound pressures is therefore a politically and socially creative resource that reorients the globe. What I am calling the vernacular is the dominant mode I am using for thinking about Black life. I turn to it because it is, I argue, the dominant mode through which global blackness notices itself and because in my view it represents the most original and resistive global Black creative life force we have yet to witness.

Forms of Black creativity are central to any consideration of Black freedom because, as I will argue, this is where we glimpse the possibility of Black freedom; those forms emerge at moments when Black people are responding to themselves, unintruded upon by the white gaze. As Dionne Brand in *A Map to the Door of No Return* has also observed, "How do I know this? Only by self-observation, only by looking. Only by feeling. Only by being a part, sitting in the room with history."[2] Only self-observation, only being observed by the self.

Black creativity is interdicted as outside of what a human life might be. Because Black creative acts are often dismissed and denigrated as outside of the realm of creativity, Black people are placed outside of modernist notions of what it means to be human. The ongoing argument that rap is not music is one example of this. But even that is conditional on how Black creativity is appropriated for the life of capital. On the one hand, such appropriations deny Black creativity while, on the other hand, in piecemeal fashion, they reward Black creativity. At the same time, such appropriations collude to kill and/or delegitimize other forms of commoditized Black creativity. The assaults against Black forms of creativity are often against the forms of creativity that are not easily or immediately capitalized/financialized or forms of creativity that suggest a sovereignty of the Black body that refuses normative ideas of freedom (e.g., the once-denigrated soul food reclaimed as an important site of the vernacular now capitalized as southern food and thereby significantly erasing the history of its Black invention). This is also the case when we think of saggin' pants, hoodies, and so on, because even when the fashion is appropriated by white middle- and working-class men, and fashion designers, the style and the attitude remain an integral element of a "Black ontology" that is not assimilable by others. It is in those moments that saggin' pants or hoodies become symbols pointing toward Black death, as in the murder of Trayvon Martin. It is such moments of incongruity that modernist logics would require us to believe are anomalies that this work investigates. That is, Black cultural creativity is appropriated for and to capital, at the same time that the Black life-form who is its author can be killed for the same creativity.

Death by violent anti-Black action and the curtailment of Black freedom are so fundamentally a part of Black life that to ignore their constitutive role is to sidestep Black life in its entirety. And yet our contemporary discourse has been to assume Black freedom has been achieved as post–civil rights inclusion and postcolonial conditions. *The Long Emancipation* refuses such inclusion as a form of freedom and instead argues that such conditions are the compromise on the way toward a freedom yet to come. I make this argument in light of the ways that ongoing Black deaths are conditioned and enacted on Black subjects when they assume the position of rights-bearing late-modern subjects. We must not fail to see that Black death and its carnage are tied to unfreedom and are a significant problem for thinking the future of all human life. But it is precisely because freedom and unfreedom have not remained central concerns of postemancipation conditions that we have mistaken emancipation for freedom and failed to acknowledge that freedom has not yet been achieved. Emancipation and postemancipation produce Black people as waste. The ease with which the Black person is killed remains central to the compromise of something that is called freedom that is not actually freedom.

Toward making this argument, I connect the Middle Passage to the Americas to the Strait of Gibraltar with the aim of orienting us to the extended time of emancipation. I argue that we are still in the time of emancipation because it has been impossible for post-"emancipation" Black people and post-"colony" Black people to both imagine and practice what an uninterdicted freedom might mean for them.

The limit of the idea of freedom as actually occurring for Black people is most clearly seen when movement happens. Our push toward freedom is marked principally by the problems that Black movement poses for nations and citizenship. Once Black people *move*, the limits of freedom and autonomy announce themselves. The brutality with which Black movement is greeted makes movement central to Black being and central to the idea of freedom that I will develop in the pages to follow. Movement in this work is actual and metaphorical: it is movement within and across borders, it is dancing, it is style, it is language, it is all the ways in which Black people attempt to express autonomy and freedom.

Walking along Checkpoint Charlie, toward the Jewish Museum in Berlin, I glimpsed some images from an art exhibition in the window of the Meyer Riegger gallery. The gallery was closed, but I was determined to return as soon as I could, given that the images that I was able to see through the window appeared to point to death in the Americas. On a subsequent visit, I sit with and pay witness to Brazilian artist Paulo Nazareth's *Genocide in Americas*. Nazareth's art asks that we encounter the Americas as a zone of death — for Black and Indigenous peoples — and his art further reminds us that such deaths are constitutive of the ways that life in the region is presently organized, lived, and experienced. Nazareth's art confirms the Americas as a zone of Black death. In what follows, I further delineate the zone of Black death and its *deathly living* as a zone where Black life-forms must persist despite or in spite of the sharp contours that continually seek to make them not thrive or exist.

In the next sections I track the ways in which Black life persists in the midst of practices, institutions, and knowledges meant to extinguish such life. I focus on the geographies of the Americas as one zone in which Black death is the foundation on which institutions, modes of being, and other forms of life stake their claims on the world. In other words, I suggest that Black death is a precondition for the commonsense knowledge and being of contemporary life. I reflect on Black death by drawing on the scholarship of Sylvia Wynter, Walter Rodney, and a range of Black radical thinkers whose intellectual projects have mapped the contours of Black resistance to premature death as a mode of remaking what it means to be human. Indeed, transatlantic slavery and, more so, the Middle Passage were routes for the invention of blackness; death — the central motif of Black life, its birth through death — is a primal constituting element of Black life-forms.

In an essay written in the aftermath of the not-guilty verdict in the trial of the police officers for brutally beating Rodney King, Sylvia Wynter reminds those of us who labor in the academy that the LAPD had a code for

FIGURE 4.1. Paulo Nazareth, *Untitled, from Cadernos de Africa project*, 2013, photo printing on cotton paper. Courtesy of the artist.

when Black suspects were encountered or involved. That code, the acronym NHI, stood for "no humans involved." Such a term can only exist because of the ways in which the foundational liberal understandings of human life place Black people outside of the category of the human. The term therefore references the central problematic of Black people in liberal humanism and the problem of a specific understanding of freedom that flows from liberalism. That such a term exists places the relationship between institutions and knowledge as central to mapping the ongoing disposability and eviction of the Black life-form from the category of human. The term's existence is evidence of the vernacular understanding that Black people are indeed a lesser life-form if not a nonhuman one entirely. Wynter's recalling of NHI and the manner in which language works to "narratively condemn" the Black also suggests Black atavism is therefore a lack of being human, as if the category of human itself is not a culturally regulating category with, therefore, the potential to change.[1] It is precisely because the human as a category is open to revision that Wynter is able to ask us to engage the university as a site to "call for a new intellectual order of knowledge that was originally made in the wake of the Civil Rights movement" to institute this "Truth."[2] In another essay, "1492: A New World View," Wynter demon-

FIGURE 4.2. Paulo Nazareth, *Antropologia do Negro II*, 2014, video. Courtesy of the artist.

strates how the category of the human evolved from one of a superstitious human to a religious human to a kind of religious/secular human. In each of these changes in what it meant to be human, we can take from Wynter a pedagogical imperative to continue to revise and reinvent what the human might be. In her call, then, that we must now undo the "narratively condemned status" of those marked as not human—that is, the Black—Wynter calls us to act in a fashion that is already available in post-Enlightenment modernist thought.[3]

The very institutionality of the Americas is a region of death for the Black life-form. In conversation with Wynter, I insist that the Americas is a region of death inaugurated by the methods of European accumulation that first make Black people legible to Europeans as a source of their own renewal and future possibilities. In so doing, land, metals, and crops all come to mark the region through the logic of economics as a zone of Black terror and death and as a zone for the ongoing assault and continuous war on Indigenous peoples. I am claiming that the Americas institutionalize terror and death as a mode of being. My attempt here is to offer a counterresponse that would be the undoing of the Americas. We might call such an undoing a decolonial struggle and a possible better future. The plantation is, I argue, in many ways the single most important aspect of the zoning of Black death. One might plausibly argue that all forms of Black terror and death lead us back to the plantation and its afterlife as the institutionality of all life and death in the Americas.

Katherine McKittrick's "Plantation Futures" helps us to see the wide-ranging institutionality of the plantation by coding or zoning it as both space and time. McKittrick's incisive critique of the ways in which plantation logics frame the past and present is an acute reading of the ways in which it operates as the site of and for "interlocking workings of modernity and blackness." McKittrick writes: "Thus, in agriculture, banking, and mining, in trade and tourism, and across other colonial and postcolonial spaces—the prison, the city, the resort—a plantation logic characteristic of (but not identical to) slavery emerges in the present both ideologically and materially."[1] McKittrick's insights point me to how the time of Black death in the zone of the Americas provides the force of life possibilities for others. Black death works to signal Black life both as waste and simultaneously as one of the sources for the production of value for others. Black life and death complicate both economic and moral understandings of what counts as value. In this sense, Black life is a challenge to normative forms of value, most evident in economic and bodily value, especially those forms of value rooted in and routed through the European Enlightenment and modernist ideals.

The plantation as the central institutionality of the zone of Black death is therefore the foundation in a larger and more dynamic production of Black life. The instantiation of the Black life-form that defies the attempt to render the laboring commodity of the slave a thing only valuable in relation to European use value offers us other modes of being human in this zone. Indeed, much of what we have come to call Black culture is a mode of living life within, against, and beyond plantation logics, which seek to thingify the Black life-form. Accrued economic use value and Black life then are crucial to the institutional foundationality that frames the death zone of the Americas.

McKittrick's "Plantation Futures" provides a foundational narrative to think agilely upon this zone as a death-dealing zone, but importantly, her argument also asks us to consider the residue of the plantation as central to the formation of its afterlife and thus as a significant and reoccurring element of contemporary life. McKittrick elsewhere suggests the epidemiological character of Black death has its lineage in the biosocial life of the plantation. Bodily health distinguishes the Black even from the African and demonstrates how the zone of the Americas invented new beings or a life-form called Black. When contemporary Africans enter this zone, they become Black and susceptible to these same conditions. Furthermore, the institution of medicine and its very foundations, from gynecology to infectious diseases, have been executed on the bodies of the Black life-form. Death is so central to blackness that it exists as the source or site to give or extend those marked as human their lives. It is precisely because Black life dies that Euro-American life is possible.

The institution of childhood is yet another example of the ways in which Black personhood is denied access to the post-Enlightenment human. The slave child was not a child; they had no childhood as such. In that absence, we might locate the institutionality of childhood as a practice and a knowledge that is always launched against, and antithetical for, the Black youthful life-form. By this I mean, and we are witnessing this in our contemporary moment, that "Black children" from the age of four onward are perceived as adultlike and therefore rendered and treated in that fashion. What is particularly crucial here is that the inability for "Black children" to be children means that all kinds of post-Enlightenment modernist institutions, practices, and knowledges can only apprehend them as antagonistic to those institutions and therefore respond to them violently. It is precisely because the slave and the afterlife of slavery do not bring the Black life-form into the category of the human that Black youthfulness can only be understood as a problem to be extinguished. These sites of antagonism—schools, the street, playgrounds, swimming pools, and more—become the terrain of Black death. Following Wynter, I understand the work of the scholar to be part of a political project in which we reorient ideas or knowledge to slip out of this yoke of Euro-American partial views of the world as the only view. To do so, I turn to the scene of Black diaspora studies to think the foundations of this dynamic further and to continually unravel its (il)logics of maiming and death.

Black diaspora is a concise conceptual and political term that is a space from which to begin to appreciate the enormity of the dispersal of those now known as Africans at a moment in European expansion and the tragic and complicated legacy of our brutal dispersal.[1] The problem of how to think diaspora as more than people and movement presents itself most powerfully in Black diaspora studies debates concerning how to assess the historical and contemporary significance of the original dispersal. But Black diaspora studies does not begin and end there. It does not begin and end in a dispersal that can only be fully understood in relation to what is now called settler colonialism and the production of Europe as ideas, geography, and people. Black diaspora studies desires to encompass a full understanding of the post-Columbus world. The dispersal that is in part set in motion by the genocide and near genocide of the Indigenous populations of the Americas has inaugurated the longest continual colonial resistance in human history. Any Black diaspora studies that does not take seriously the genocide and near genocide of Indigenous populations of the Americas alongside the commencement of African transatlantic slavery is, in my view, a diaspora studies not worth having at all.

At the same time, any conceptual and discursive rendering of settler colonialism that does not seriously grapple with the far-reaching brutality of the invention of Black beings/the Black life-form is a politics and study not worth having. Sylvia Wynter's numerous essays are central to thinking on the European invention and proliferation of a "New World" (view) that European Enlightenment expansion ushered in for all of us. Central to the idea of the "New World" (view) is, I believe, an understanding of the geopolitics of economy and the geopolitics of modernity's imaginary sphere that have followed in the wake of Europe's expansion into worlds it previously had not known — those worlds we have come to call in such fashion the Americas. Part of the story here is how discourses of coloniality have come to mark and determine even the ways in which we have dealt with these conceptual and material turns so that terms like *diaspora* can sometimes come to conceal crucial and important links and contexts for the materiality that diaspora also seeks to capture in its conceptual and political range. The disappearance of Indigenous peoples from diaspora conversations is a case in point. When one puts slavery in relation to Indigenous genocide and ongoing colonization, one gets the expanded conception of diaspora that I am elaborating. For example, Bartolomé de Las Casas, in his book *A Short Account of the Destruction of the Indies*, upon his reckoning with the decimation of Indigenous peoples, arrives at the conclusion that they possessed souls and could therefore be saved and Christianized. He understood his new perspective as one that should free Indigenous peoples from enslavement at the same time that he articulated that Africans lacked a soul and therefore would make perfect slaves in the early extractive economies of the Americas.[2] It is examples like this that necessitate that we think settler colonialism and transatlantic slavery together because they are bound together in that discourse. The conception of diaspora that I am working with is a radical engagement with the category of the human and with an order of knowledge and a worldview complicated by the creative conditions of a Black discrepant modernity produced in the Americas from the myriad encounters of worldviews brutally cohering together, in contradiction and mutuality, to produce continually a different people since 1492.[3] The politically contentious phrase *New World* does hold both a negative and a positive possibility and potentiality.

Transatlantic slavery is more than a political-economic phenomenon; it is more than the history of early capitalist accumulation; it is a seismic human cultural shift in economy, thought, and culture and, thus, in human alterability.[4] Transatlantic slavery along with the brutal theft of Indigenous territories is the engine that has driven capitalism and its various global incarnations for the past five hundred years. The manner in which European, and indeed global, thought changed in the context of transatlantic slavery beyond that of the political-economic phenomenon should be immediately evident to most.[5] However, slavery's utterance only seems to be heard at the juncture of political economy as though that is the beginning and the end. Instead, we need to think about transatlantic slavery and Indigenous colonization as a cultural revolution that is still unfolding in ways that remain deeply traumatic and must be reckoned with. Such a reckoning cannot be one in which we merely pinpoint victims and victimizers; it must grapple with the complicated entanglements of historical and contemporary implications in each other's lives that range from Cherokee enslavement of Black beings to Barack Obama as the president of a white supremacist settler colonial nation.[6] Recognizing the complications and "the intervention of history," as Stuart Hall puts it, can help us to better work with the still-unfolding impact of Indigenous colonization and transatlantic slavery.[7] When Hall uses the phrase "the intervention of history," he's often pointing to the ways in which the making of historical conditions is used to intervene in situations in which complicated entanglements are not easily pulled apart, such as the examples provided earlier. Hall says that history intervenes, making the attempt to disentangle not useful—instead we might proceed from the present juncture of entanglement. Following Wynter, we might understand 1492 and transatlantic slavery as ushering in new forms of human and social life in which the European comes to name and order the world on the terms of their cosmopolitical, religio-social worldview—or, more plainly, European cultural foundations of their knowledge systems.

Thus, in my view, Black diaspora studies is implicated both in the unraveling of this "New World" (view), which, as Walter Mignolo states, involves the "control of money, and control of meaning and being are parallel processes," and in Europe's reordering of the globe on its Judeo-Christian philosophical terms.[8] From this perspective, Black diaspora studies is concerned with the remaking and the resignifying of the category of the human beyond the boundaries imposed on it in a post-1492 worldview for which revisions have been made through and by a host of various political and cultural struggles.[9] The fundamental question and concern of Black diaspora studies, it seems to me, should be to make sense of, to analyze what the events of 1492 and their aftermath set into motion, and how various configurations of peoples—Indigenous and Black—have contested with and been shaped by these events.

Why diaspora? This is a question that concerns the politics of history and the ways that such politics and histories can be mobilized for a freedom still to come. In this regard, historians of the Atlantic seem to have reached a crucially important place in their debates—the recognition of how the impact of European expansion has reshaped the globe on Euro-Western terms.[10] The ideas birthed in the context of the Atlantic world have been central to the ways in which European coloniality spread its global reach and thus the ways in which many other diasporas have come into being. (Here I am thinking about the Indian, Chinese, Arab, and early Jewish diasporas in the New World.) Peter Linebaugh and Marcus Rediker's rather useful metaphor of the "many-headed hydra" is apt for thinking the historical and contemporary peregrinations of Euro-Western reordering of the globe post-1492.[11] In this regard, capitalism as an organizing structure and new emergent ideas about humanness converge as the most salient examples of that reshaping. Atlantic historians have been front and center in demonstrating the global historical reach and impact of both economy and culture, and how, in fact, the two might indeed be one.

Much of the debate in Black diaspora studies has been about what some see as too central a focus on the Atlantic world, in essence a juggling for comparative equality of seas. Critics who believe that the Atlantic is too central to diaspora studies will often offer the Pacific and the Indian Oceans as countermodels of dispersal. What these counters fail to fully account for is that the Atlantic model was adapted and deployed in those spaces as well. In the more than two decades since the publication of Paul Gilroy's book *The Black Atlantic*, the desire to displace the Atlantic as foundational to Black diaspora studies has been a constant.[1] There is, it seems to me, a fundamental misunderstanding at work in the debate. To insist on the world-changing impact of the ongoing colonization of the Americas and transatlantic slavery as central to Black diaspora studies is neither to argue for exceptionalism nor to produce a singular grand narrative of modernity's birth. In *Modernity Disavowed: Haiti and the Cultures of Slavery in the Age of Revolution*, Sibylle Fischer writes, "Heterogeneity is a congenital condition of modernity."[2] Fischer further argues:

> If we do not take into account to what extent modernity is a product of the New World, to what extent the colonial experience shaped modernity—in Europe and elsewhere—politically, economically, and aesthetically, and to what extent modernity is a heterogeneous, internally diverse, even contradictory phenomenon that constituted and revolutionized itself in the process of transculturation, then, obviously, talk of modernity is just a reinstantiation of a Eurocentric particularism parading as universalism.[3]

I find in Fischer an important point of departure for thinking about 1492 and transatlantic slavery in the context of debates concerning diaspora, transnationalism, and settler colonialism. Fischer allows me to think of the ways in which the Atlantic zone functions to put in place the mechanisms for the production of the resources (material, intellectual, and otherwise) for Europe to make its global play. Hence, the position Fischer stakes out runs counter to the kind of critique that has for so long been the mainstay of Black diaspora studies and its Atlantic refusal.

Take, for example, Paul Zeleza's critique of Paul Gilroy, in which he suggests that "the studies of diasporic agency and originality" are valorized. Zeleza correctly acknowledges that Gilroy's version is only one part of a complicated and entangled context that comes to be read as the whole. Zeleza faults "cosmopolitan intellectuals" for peddling such analyses, not mentioning that *he too might be read* within that group, as he reports that he travels with a Canadian passport, resides in the United States, and travels to Africa often, making him a member of what he terms the "new or contemporary African diaspora."[4] But even more important, it might have been useful to Zeleza's critique of Gilroy if he had at least positioned continental Africans' complicated complicity with the production of the "New World," as Saidiya Hartman's *Lose Your Mother* has so brilliantly accomplished.[5] We might claim that not all movement across borders makes a diaspora, and while it is politically useful to make crucial distinctions about forms of migration, the Black beings on whom the ideas of antiblackness have been invented have no easy shores to return to—we have a *deathly living* in the zone of the Americas.

Reading Hartman, Gilroy, and Zeleza together, one comes up against the stakes of Black movement. In Gilroy and Hartman, the central problematic of Black movement concerns itself with the ways in which both the natal break with Africa (Hartman) and the production of new Black selves in the Americas (Gilroy and Hartman) register differently from the particular contemporary classed movement of Zeleza. Nonetheless, there is a link between these movements, which centers on the question of knowledge and institutions, by which I mean that Black diaspora thought allows us to see the ways that knowledge circulates to form communities beyond the social relations of familial kinship. Both Hartman and Gilroy unpack the implications of knowledge as kinship and its accompanying dissonances, terrors, and undoings, while Zeleza does a reading of knowledge that seeks to reconstitute a very particular and knowable Africa.

These differences position the North Atlantic academy in a sphere of power for which our studies should attempt to mean something. It means not letting the university off the hook as a crucial link in global capitalism's domination in Euro-Western guise because ideas have been the central ingredient in the geopolitics of the globe in the past five hundred years. A Black diaspora thought that begins with the European attempt to conquer the Americas and the inauguration of transatlantic slavery limits nothing; it opens up all the avenues for a more honest global conversation about what that expansion set in motion. Furthermore, such Black diaspora studies should not step away from the difficult debate of making life in a place where the ethics of arrival can be fashioned through the brutal thefts of Euro-Western dominance and claims to restore their stewardship of the lands. How might Black diaspora studies, taking as central transatlantic slavery's invention of Black beings, engage the further dynamics of Black ontologies in the Americas and Africa?

It is my argument that a Black diaspora studies might/will take us a long way toward refusing and offering better analyses of institutional and corporate multiculturalisms that mobilize difference as a commodity for corporate munificence. Additionally, Black diaspora studies can be a buttress against a postcolonial studies and a transnational and globalization studies that refuse to complicate the tensions between old and new colonialisms and the ways in which empire in its old and new forms might be situated in a discontinuous continuum of Euro-Western ethno-domination. Significantly, diaspora thought allows us to confront and engage the difficult and violent politics of modernity's invention of the nation-state and the nation-state's inability to produce a space for the full expression of human possibility. Instead, the nation-state provides ethnocultural identities as the basis of an imagined care for the self that always seems to fall short of full human status and expression, thus always requiring Black people to keep moving.

It seems to me that part of what it means to speak of a Black diaspora is to account for the ways in which return to an imagined or real homeland is always foreclosed and profoundly impossible. The impossibility is conditioned by the brutal dispersal along with the severe cultural interruptions and the intervention of history that brought new attachments, subjectivities, and identifications into being or formation. At the same time, those conditions make belonging to nations brutally and totally impossible. Thus, not all contemporary continental African migration might or can count as diasporic, even though a certain political logic requires it to be so given the all-encompassing logics and practices of anti-Black formations in the West. There is a qualitative difference between the now clear impossibility of return for, say, many Somalis and that of, let's say, some (white) South Africans. Such claims are difficult evaluative ones to make, but taken within a rubric of cultural identity and the very materiality of the nation-state as a point of return, making the evaluation is useful even if it still does have some unresolved fault lines in its conceptuality. The primary issue to consider nonetheless is how the *longue dureé* of Euro-Western domination has impacted the complicated postcolonial politics set in motion through the events of the past five hundred–plus years, which continue to produce new subjects for the Black diaspora out of a post-1492 and postcolonial Africa. Our debates have so far failed to adequately think those moments and conditions.

The Atlantic region—with its history of territorial theft, transatlantic slavery, and genocide—is the *incubator* of a set of conditions that we have inherited as a global situation organized on the basis of Euro-Western traditions of thought and the human, and from which we must figure out how to extricate ourselves. I am not suggesting that language and regions are not important to these concerns. A sober conversation about what extrication means must take on political economy, cultural borrowing, sharing, mixing, and its outcomes and impacts—contradictory, antagonistic, and otherwise. Such a conversation must also contend with our entangled histories of power, knowledge, and land.

A radical Black diaspora studies/thought should seriously engage conversations concerning the Atlantic region because the social and cultural revisions of the past five hundred years have produced asymmetrical positions that allow for a kind of "racial contract" based on class and gender by or through which some Black people can enter a revised Euro-Western body politic.[6] The same cannot be said for the large masses of Indigenous peoples whom many still like to think of as extinct or in the past, especially in parts of the Caribbean. Black diaspora politics might be about something—how land, power, and knowledge have come together to enact and unfold one of the longest unbroken colonial periods in human history. It might also provide a better explanation of the past and the ways that current conceptions of the present find their sustenance in the past—ideologically and otherwise.

The Americas and the African continent offer different and difficult focal points in this debate. Africa remains a troubling place of Black diaspora identification. The story of Africa is a complex one for "New World" Black people who make use of Africa and also "make Africa" in numerous ways.[7] The making of and coming to terms with Africa in the "New World" is of particular importance to my thinking. As Jamaica Kincaid has presciently written about Caribbean peoples in *Harper's* magazine, they are a people who must make themselves native to a place they are not from.[8] Concomitant with this making is the near genocide of the Taino and the Caribs and the brutal evidence of transatlantic slavery. Stacking Kincaid's claim next to the various African states' apologies for slavery complicates the picture. The public relations impact of such an apology simultaneously limns the rupture of and the desire for a "New World" reconnection with Africa, at the same time that it reinstates the foundational importance of transatlantic slavery to a Black global body politic. It is a suture that continually erupts and sutures again. The discursive effects of such apologies are the recognition of the ongoing tremors of transatlantic slavery on the continent and in the diaspora.

For diaspora studies, the consequences of ignoring 1492 and transatlantic slavery are serious and many. But since I have been mainly interested in addressing this argument to the institutional imperatives of producing knowledge in the university, let me more clearly mark the institutions of concern. Diaspora programs, centers, conferences, and seminars are springing up everywhere these days. The surfeit of institutions is fueled by the older and newer migratory populations—forced, planned, and unplanned. In fact, the post-1492 world has bequeathed the massive shifts in population around the globe in its aftermath, the first such movement being transatlantic slavery and continuing since. As Toni Morrison writes in "Home":

> The overweening, defining event of the modern world is the mass movement of raced populations, beginning with the largest forced transfer of people in the history of the world: slavery. The consequences of which transfer have determined all the wars following it as well as the current ones being waged on every continent. The contemporary world's work has become policing, halting, forming policy regarding, and trying to administer the movement of people. Nationhood—the very definition of citizenship—is constantly being demarcated and redemarcated in response to exiles, refugees, Gastarbeiter, immigrants, migrations, the displaced, the fleeing, and the besieged. The anxiety of belonging is entombed within the central metaphors in the discourse on globalism, transnationalism, nationalism, the break-up of federations, the rescheduling of alliances, and the fictions of sovereignty.[9]

Conceptually, Black diaspora must grapple with the central claim of the European Enlightenment and modernity—to make a better human, one that is fundamentally, always, positioned against the Black and indeed is dependent on the logics of antiblackness that produce Black beings as nonhuman. The work is to make that claim foundational for Black diaspora studies/thought because it is, in fact, the various ways in which deployments of Western conceptions of the human function that continue to be the basis from which diasporic sensibilities, consciousness, and a potential politics might arise.

In the case of "New World Blacks," the impossibility of any return, imagined or real (even when individuals and groups physically return), means that the break that transatlantic slavery produced for some people, who identify with Africa, is an identification that can only be sutured through various and different kinds of performances of politics that place Africa within their discursive reach and imagination.[10]

Derek Walcott's divided tongue best captures the actual place of Africa when he asks rhetorically in "A Far Cry from Africa": "How choose between this Africa and the English tongue I love?"[11] But he also furnishes that divided tongue, or the representation of the self, with an insistence on a hopeful self (in a later work, "The Schooner Flight") who has "no nation now but the imagination," allowing for a world citizenship that entangles, implicates, and complicates anew by refusing one of modernity's central inventions: the nation-state.[12] By so doing, Walcott offers a useful lens from which to make reparation with the ongoing traumas of a world reconfigured on the basis of Euro-Western terms. Walcott seizes the moment to reside in the interstices of an evolving sensibility and reality.

When C. L. R. James wrote about the economics of lynching and its uneven geographies in the 1940s as the United States prepared to join the Second World War, he pointed to the contradictions that surrounded lynching. He argued that much lynching did not occur in places where white employers relied on Black labor because white employers wanted to ensure they had a workforce; in other places, lynching took place by the white working class who saw Black labor as a competitive threat to their economic and cultural prospects. Thus, in the latter areas, lynching was not only economic but also cultural, and white racial bonding was produced through the logics of post-Enlightenment and modern practices meant to render the "negro" outside the national family as a group who could share in the national resources. In this regard, I think of Rosewood (documented in John Singleton's film of the same name), a Black town and community in Florida in which one of the most horrific stories of lynching, terrorism, and the massacre of Black life took place. Rosewood was an autonomous Black community, but its white "neighbors" felt it had to be kept in its place, not so much because it was a force of economic competition but because its very existence challenged the foundational logics of white supremacy. By this I mean, the very autonomy that is supposed to be the modern liberal perfection of the human and that is often measured by economic success is the very thing that when performed by Black beings inaugurates white violence. James is clear that the state responded differently to lynchings depending on what was at stake. In instances where labor was needed for the war effort, the state acted. In areas where no such labor was needed, the state looked the other way or supported the actions of the white mobs. What James demonstrates with his reading of divided lynching is that the link between the economic and the cultural cannot be easily divided. James wants us to acknowledge the contradiction that lies at various settlements in time when the state will protect Black life and at other times when the state will become a party to its extinguishment. James helps us to account for the ways in which Black death is central to the very foundations of the modern nation-state and specifically its capitalist formations—via plantation genocidal logics and practices.

I have been thinking about how the Zones of Black Death have produced new states of being for Black life-forms. These states of being are fundamentally premised on practices of what Houston A. Baker Jr. called, in the context of African American literature, "mastery of form and deformation of mastery."[1] I turn to Baker to flesh out how Black life-forms survive by both mastering the conditions under which life proceeds and simultaneously deforming those conditions so that they might have access to selves beyond the degrading violence of everyday life. The earlier example of lynching, in which James points out that lynching might and might not be connected to labor or the economy, demonstrates that Black people had to master and deform the social relations of white supremacy as a structure of survival. It is precisely the manner in which Black life deforms and reforms (and not in the liberal democratic sense of abeyance to already established institutional forms) in completely radical ways the foundational claims of post-Enlightenment modernity that Black people remain killable. To return to Rosewood, the assault on and destruction of that Black town emerged from white supremacy's inability to acknowledge that Black people practiced forms of modernity that white people believed they had no intellectual capacity for or ability to access. Black life-forms' placement outside the category of the human is the foundational root and route of Euro-American humanity coming into being. Black life is the residue of the failed and flawed ideals of a modernist humanism that itself could only be made possible through the denigration of Black life.

Old pirates, yes, they rob I,
Sold I to the merchant ships,
Minutes after they took I
From the bottomless pit.
—BOB MARLEY, "Redemption Song," from *Uprising* (1980)

Migration. Can it be called migration? There is a sense of return in migrations—a sense of continuities, remembered homes—as with birds or butterflies or deer or fish. Those returns which are lodged indelibly, unconsciously, instinctively in the mind. But migrations suggest intentions or purposes. Some choice and, if not choice, decisions. And if not decisions, options, all be they difficult. But the sense of return in the Door of No Return is one of irrecoverable losses of those very things which make returning possible. A place to return to, a way of being, familiar sights or sounds, familiar smells, a welcome perhaps, but a place, welcome or not.
— DIONNE BRAND, *A Map to the Door of No Return: Notes to Belonging* (2001)

Movement is central to the shape of the modern world: whether post-Columbus European expansion around the globe, the movement of millions of Africans into the Americas, or the expropriation and movement of millions of Indigenous peoples from their traditional lands. Movement was also one of the central problematics of emancipated ex-enslaved Black people. At the heart of migration and citizenship sit the questions of emancipation and freedom. Recent events in Europe and the Americas make such a claim exceedingly clear.[1] One cannot help but think about the ways that people's movements now sit as one of the central problematics of late neoliberal capitalist arrangements. In fact, postslavery movements of all kinds are conditioned by the afterlife of slavery and more specifically by the twentieth-century anti-Black migration policies of the West. It is precisely because the ex-enslaved refused to remain on plantations that Asian indentureship became a central postslavery phenomenon. Black people or the ex-enslaved began to move around internally and externally as an element of their newly emancipated selves. That movement opened up a new era of post-transatlantic migrations. African "transshipped" peoples' movement became central to the modern and late-modern world.[2] The ability to move, then, became a central dynamic of freedom in a postslavery world. This movement was not merely within already-set borders (like the movement of millions of Black people from South to North within the United States) but was also beyond borders in the Caribbean archipelago.

It is not surprising that at yet another moment of significant crisis, this time in neoliberal capitalism, Black movement has retained its animating force concerning questions of nation, citizenship, and freedom. Indeed, despite claims otherwise, the emancipation of those enslaved in both the then British Empire and the United States (1834/1838 and 1865, respectively) was considered first a crisis of capital and then a significant social and cultural problem. Plantations and slaveholders in both places were monetarily compensated for their "loss." The compensation to former slave owners marks a significant element of the juridical process of emancipation bringing contract law and monetary policy into the equation, further cementing my claim that emancipation is not freedom. Freedom is extralegislative— freedom exists beyond the confines of the law as a mode of experiencing life without bounds. The logics of transatlantic slavery continue to shape Black movement and, therefore, Black belonging globally. My particular concern is with the ways that Black movements, since the period of transatlantic slavery, have been circumscribed and animated by a desire for freedom and halted by the realities of brutal deaths. These deaths are occasioned by the limits of the nation-state to provide avenues of and for citizenship that might appear to move toward the promise of freedom for Black subjects or what I have come to call the Black life-form. Situating the nation-state as central to the legacy of transatlantic slavery and its afterlives unsettles settlement, citizenship, and nation. My attention to situating Black life and its deathly limits within the legal process of emancipation is to accentuate the difference between emancipation and freedom and the ways in which the legislative practices of statecraft work to make impossible Black citizenship and even Black belonging in nations, especially those designated Western.

The tension and difference between the idea of emancipation and the idea of freedom is captured in part by Bob Marley's "Redemption Song." The song is a masterpiece of analysis because in its moving from the hold of the ship to atomic energy it is able, through the economy of the lyric, to capture the period from African enslavement to late modernity with its potential nuclear implosion while demonstrating the discontinuous continuity that constitutes one historical period. In "Redemption Song," freedom and emancipation are in a tense relationship. Emancipation is a prior moment to being able to sing songs of freedom, but first minds must be emancipated from mental slavery. Marley invokes emancipation and freedom as entangled elements of everyday life but, most important, as the metapractices that shape how we might respond to the world around us. Still in a period of emancipation — the long emancipation — it is the question of unfreedom that animates my thinking here. Marley's call for emancipation from mental slavery echoes the concern that freedom has not yet been achieved. *Freedom is still in advance of our desires.* As we attempt to bring to a conclusion this long process of emancipation, a process that is temporally different in different parts of the world — the Spanish and Portuguese in Cuba (1886) and Brazil (1888) emancipated the Black enslaved later than the English, the French, and the Americans — freedom remains elusive. "Illegal" forms of slavery existed much longer than the temporal period of legal emancipation. The image-archive of post-Columbus slavery even finds resonance in photographs coming from the continued intractability of Euro-American global empire ongoing in Libya and the postwar exposure of the Black enslaved there.

The legal parameters of emancipation in each region were different, but in no instance did emancipation give the formerly enslaved the right simply to leave their surroundings. Attempts by the formerly enslaved to exercise any form of freedom are met with a torrent of laws that extend the enclosure: laws against idleness, vagrancy, or noise; pass laws, and so on. The potential for freedom begins, one might argue, in two parts: first the refusal of apprenticeship and second the refusal to remain on plantations. Taken together, those two refusals were the first salvo in an articulation of postslavery freedom that then had to be interrupted. Laws restricting Black movement quickly became central to postslave societies buttressed by tremendous forms of violent enforcement. The point at which freedom of movement is expressed and acted on by the formerly enslaved reveals the limits of emancipation. In such instances, the law asserts itself to reinstate emancipation as a process and an unfinished project that could have been one of moving toward freedom. In fact, the British emancipation act was not repealed until 1998 in a cleanup of English statute law. What the cleanup did leave in place, however, was antislavery legislation that was heavily influenced by, or premised on, the "new" language of antitrafficking laws.

In each instance in the contemporary where concerns about migration take center stage, the Black body, the Black life-form, is read as abundant to the problem. Whether we are thinking of fortress Europe or the gates/borders/walls of North America, the specter of the Black life-form entering plays a significant role in state policy marking migration and citizenship. While in the popular media in the United States, migration or migrants are often understood to be Latinx and read, therefore, as not Black, the reality is far more complex. In both the United States and Canada, large numbers of Black-identified people exist as "undocumented aliens" (and many of them are Latinx). The large numbers of non-Black Latinx people who have organized and made their desires public have provided a screen to make invisible Black others, including those Afro-Latinx people who organized with them. One must be clear, however, that it is their existence and presence that often fuel state policies on migration meant to hold Black populations in stasis in North America. Dating back to the turn of the twentieth century, Canada has had a history of anti-Black migratory practices wherein Black people were "deemed unsuitable" for entry, existence, and citizenship. In fact, many of the post–September 11, 2001, enhanced immigration policies build on earlier policies put in place to limit and demarcate Black migration. Put another way, historically and presently, most North American and European migration policies have been framed on keeping blackness out in order to locate blackness as the constituent outside, and to limit the numbers within.

To more fully account for Black movement in the contemporary world, we might want to spend some time thinking with Walter Rodney's book *How Europe Underdeveloped Africa*. The force of Rodney's argument is that colonial management coupled with the history of transatlantic slavery produced within Africa the very conditions that prohibited its development on the terms that the West states are the terms of development. The carving up of Africa in 1884 and the prior theft of its peoples continue to shape the continent's registers of life. Rodney's critique of colonial power remains useful despite some critics' claims that it is a too-simple analysis. In fact, reading Rodney alongside Sylvia Wynter, one sees more clearly the ways that the logics of development are decidedly cast against Africa and blackness. One sees that the project of development in a still-colonial globe means that even with the contemporary discourse of "Africa rising," Africa will remain perpetually "underdeveloped" and "behind."[3] Thus, the desire of Africans to leave the continent, as evidenced by the crossing of the Mediterranean at the Strait of Gibraltar, is a crucial and not surprising outcome of a history of what Rodney termed "planned and unplanned" migration for African peoples. The ejection of Africans and their subsequent migration are a direct result of those planned underdevelopment policies. It should be clear from this argument that Africa is a central part of the long emancipation, since independence from former colonial masters has not reshaped global relations in ways that we might call freedom. In fact, the ongoing global colonial relations are the central backdrop for why some Africans need to move, because postcolonial independence is a continuation of juridical and legislative emancipation. While some might suggest that the postcolonies of Africa are not ex-enslaved colonies and therefore the language of emancipation does not apply, I suggest that the nature of the colonialism that produced those postcolonial states is in part also the lineage of transatlantic slavery. In the Americas we get freed, and in Africa they get independence.

If we join Rodney's thought with Fanon's and Wynter's, we see everywhere that the "bio-evolutionary dysselected peoples of African and Afromixed descent" find themselves marked as outsiders.[4] Thus, the question of citizenship bears a weightiness in regard to one's proximity to those marked as dysselected peoples and to "their degrees of nearness to or distance from its signifier status as the ultimate marker of genetic non-being."[5] This is why a phenotypically "white-looking" Latinx person can become the face of the migrant movement in the United States and Canada. In short, the logics of anti-Black racism structure even the resistance to migratory regulations in our time. In order to adequately gauge these disturbing conditions of Black being, we must be able to notice the severe limits that everywhere mark the Black life-forms' conditions of possibility. The limited boundaries provided by emancipation and postcolonial nation-states mean that Black migratory practices occasion the breaking of those boundaries of confinement and containment, and open up new possibilities.

The project of Black movement, however, is not only conditioned by African or Black enslavement and continental exploitation and "underdevelopment." Black movement is also conditioned by global articulations of race and blackness conceived in the time of transatlantic slavery and African colonization and partition. Jemima Pierre's book *The Predicament of Blackness*, an anthropological study of race in Ghana, demonstrates persuasively that global ideas of race, racism, blackness, and whiteness permeate the African continent in ways, for example, that are both similar to and different from New World blackness. Pierre's argument suggests that only faulty thinking takes Africa outside of the global logics of race. Using the

FIGURE 9.1. Libyan coastguardsman stands on boat during rescue of immigrants, 2017. Photo by Taha Jawashi/AFP; courtesy of Getty Images.

way in which the language of the "native" comes to take center stage in the African colonial project, she highlights how the word *native* works to racialize Black people into subordinate and inferior roles: "Nativization was racialization but this racialization worked through *ethnicization*—the constitution and reorganization of a constellation of tribal groupings whose incorporation into colonial society depended on mediating its racial and cultural separation from the 'civil' and 'civilized' society of White European colonizers."[6] Colonial Ghana was structured through forms of segregation, pass laws, and all the other forms of racialization that marked the slaveholding Americas. Thus, the idea that race and racialization were not a part of the African colonial project is a rather odd one that has nonetheless had much currency over the years. But equally important, Pierre shows how the mark of "native" came to serve larger social, cultural, and economic contexts that in the long run also helped to produce the push toward migration for some Africans both past and present. Taking Pierre alongside Rodney and Wynter, we get the full force of the conditions that mark Black/African movement around the globe. Those conditions—economic, cultural, social, and otherwise—constitute the belly of European colonial practices and the reordering of the globe on their own terms as the only terms for living a life.

FIGURE 9.2. Group of people who claim to be Haitian prepare to cross the border from New York into Canada, 2017. Photo by Geoff Robins/AFP; courtesy of Getty Images.

Stuart Hall writes that "migration is the joker in the globalization pack" and that both planned and unplanned migrations demonstrate that "migrants have an ambivalent position in contemporary globalization."[7] Hall sums up the problematics of contemporary migration in this way:

> Migration constitutes a disruptive force with globalization. Unlike earlier phases, where the problems of religious, social, and cultural difference were held at a safe distance from metropolitan homelands, contemporary migration intrudes directly into, disturbs, challenges, and subverts, metropolitan cultural space. It projects the vexed issue of pluralism and difference into the epistemic rupture, generating the thematics of a new problematic—that of the postcolonial moment.[8]

It is postcolonial pushes of various sorts, from poverty to war to economic adjustments and trade imbalances, that have further occasioned the refining of migratory policies aimed now at "returning" or fixing the formerly colonized in their place so that, as Hall states: "Only labor—people—are supposed to stay still."[9] And yet people move despite the significant attempts to hold them in their places, "a sort of deregulated globalization-from-below."[10] In places such as Canada, where Temporary Foreign Worker Programs are significant, labor moves in and under very proscribed terms. The fear for neoliberal politicians and late capitalism is that such "moving" labor might become unruly; thus, its numbers are limited. Asylum seekers, migrant labor, illegal, undocumented, dreamers, refugees, *sans papiers* are some of the ways in which, for some, relations to the nation-state and the lack of citizenship are marked. But it is precisely because the state remains the arbiter of citizenship and because citizenship suggests settlement that these forms of naming mark a relational condition to the state and remain wholly inadequate for what is being experienced in this moment of global crisis. These names and conditions mark the insufficiency of the nation-state as an avatar for producing Black life and instead point to it as a site of multiple violences.

In his articulation of tidalectics, Edward Kamau Brathwaite has argued that Caribbean culture is a submerged culture. From Lampedusa, Italy, to the Caribbean Sea, Black life is submerged culture because of the multiple ways in which its watery existence comes into being. The question of the ship, already prefigured in these pages by Wynter's "transshipped culture," brings with it the dreaded possibilities of death. But Brathwaite refuses to take death as finality.[1] Instead, he offers the submerged as a double articulation of death, catastrophe, and a rebirth that requires that we rethink the very terms of life itself. The submerged culture is neither a counterculture nor an alternative culture, but a living critique of the past and the present.

The Haitian movement in the Caribbean Sea has caused panic for the "Black" island nations of that region and the United States and even Canada. One reason is because the submerged memories of transatlantic slavery's horrors surface as still present to the region of the Americas, and Haiti's historic revolution remains a repressed event of the death zone of the Americas. The movement of these Haitians finds its corollary in the African crossings of the Mediterranean Sea to Lampedusa, Italy. The crossing of the Strait of Gibraltar by Africans has been characterized as a second Middle Passage. In the long emancipation, such crossings are an extension of the Middle Passage and are not a new Middle Passage. Indeed, the Middle Passage cannot be pluralized; its uniqueness as the ongoing project of coloniality demands otherwise. If we take seriously Rodney's claim of the underdevelopment of Africa due to transatlantic slavery and colonial theft, we are able to see, as uniquely its own, the extensions and evidence of the Middle Passage into the present.

As Sylvia Wynter argues, in her unmaking of the notion of "natural scarcity": "These archipelagoes of joblessness and poverty function at a world-systemic level as the chaos to our First World 'developed' societies, in as lawlike a manner as the inner cities' dystopia negates the behavior-orienting goal of the 'affluent pursuit of happiness' of those who live in the utopia of the suburbs."[2] It is the lawlike practices, not just the laws, that continually fashion a certain Black out-of-placeness everywhere, and those practices are the basis of migratory practices and policies in the "developed" West. Those practices have their foundational originality in the ongoing long emancipation from transatlantic slavery to the present now governed by the laws of movement globally constituted out of and by old and new empires.

Three interlocking ideas or concepts have been useful for me to think through this problem: catastrophe, the wake, and hauntology. Together, these concepts allow us to access something about how anti-Black logics of the globe shape the ways in which Black life-forms are prohibited from citizenship and belonging in nations. These three ideas make sense of the broader dynamics of how blackness has been globalized as the life-form to be avoided or, as Frank B. Wilderson terms it, "always already void of relationality."[3] Kamau Brathwaite further develops his articulation of submerged culture in what he calls the literature of catastrophe. I replace *literature* with *culture* in order to argue that culture of catastrophe signals the deadly arrival of Africans in the Americas and the life that comes from crossing the Middle Passage or Atlantic into a new world. The *deadly living* that comes of that crossing and its resultant histories of survival provide the template for the long emancipation. Emancipation was and is a compromise meant to retain control over Black bodies, Black life-forms, and our movement while appearing to offer significantly changed conditions from those of enslavement and colonization. The struggle was for freedom, *not* emancipation, and it began before the slave ships left the African coast.

Importantly, then, Christina Sharpe's articulation of "the wake" adds immeasurably to my proposition of the culture of catastrophe because it allows us the respite to meditate on the *longue dureé* of moving toward freedom. Sharpe's articulation and formulation of the wake require that we grapple with death, with the necessary and functional Black dead as the resource toward making modernity and capitalism. Sharpe tells us, in conversation with Saidiya Hartman, that

> to encounter people of African descent in the wake both materially and as a problem for thought is to encounter that * in the grand narrative of history; and, in the conditions of Black life and death such as those delineated by Hartman ("skewed life chances, limited access to health and education, premature death") and the ways we are po-

sitioned through and by them, the ways we occupy the "I" of Hartman's "I am the afterlife of slavery" (Hartman 2008, 6).[4]

The signal importance of Sharpe taking up the concept of the wake is that it contends with the work that Black death does in this world. Asking if the Black womb is a tomb, Sharpe prefigures Black life as almost always already dead in a postslavery world that continually finds Black people to be out-of-place and waste. To be in the wake, then, is to live in the desire to work toward freedom in the face of death. And yet Sharpe's articulation reaches beyond the pessimistic to provide us with a conceptual turn that allows us also to mark the cultures that Black people make as forms of life with death. The practice of the Black wake is about more than death. In the moment of death, the wake works to honor lives lived and to provide a conduit for those left behind so that life might be experienced as more than merely that of subjection.

The culture of catastrophe, as one lives in the wake, moving toward freedom, might be understood as a hauntology. Jacques Derrida, in concert with Sharpe, argues that the learning of life is "only from the other and by death."[5] Derrida, in *Specters of Marx*, is an excellent companion for Brathwaite and Sharpe, since his concern with specters is also concern with "a *politics* of memory, of inheritance, and of generation."[6] Both Brathwaite and Sharpe take memory and inheritance seriously as powerful points to and for Black life. It is precisely the ways in which legacies of the past condition present circumstances that allow for Black lives to exist in a space of unbelievability. Derrida reminds us as he moves toward, but does not arrive at, a definition of hauntology that the ghost is both an event and a first time, but, importantly, it is also a repetition.

The simultaneous value and lack of value for Black life, hinted at earlier in my discussion of James and lynching, is most evident in the ways that Black people, their bodies, and their practices are spectacularized. Following Derrida, it is at the point of event and repetition that Black life is made both present and unbelievable. Black life generally finds itself in a repeated cycle of being spectacularized, often through visual representations in popular culture (found in sport, in music, on social media, in memes and GIFs, in movies, etc.). At the same time, and more specifically, the state violence that is repeatedly inflicted on Black people is seen as otherworldly and somehow not believable. And yet, this repeated spectacularization of violent events occasions a frenzied gaze and the repeated viewing of the brutality inflicted by non-Black people on Black people. Black people bear witness to this disbelief with the certainty that, for example, the police who murder Black people or those white people protected by "stand your ground" laws in the United States will not be convicted even as their acts of violence are spectacularly displayed on our collective screens. The video-recorded evidence and the body of the dead Black person are not enough to secure belief that what has taken place is, in fact, a murder. Thus, through a logic of disbelief, Black life is produced as both immediately present and immediately absent — appeared and disappeared.

HOW DID OUR SLAVE past become our emancipated, neoliberal present? Because we are not yet free, our slave past haunts and mars our attempt to render the past as past and the foundation for a future to come. The persistence of the past announces itself in discourses and practices of diversity, equity, multiculturalism, and antiracism policies, all of which can be tied to the logics of legislative emancipation's juridical form. This, too, is the long emancipation. Those modes of adaptation that are often embraced as transformation and change meant to signal the shifting foundational arrangements of our societies are actually grounded in the extended logic of the terms and conditions juridical emancipation set out for Black life. These terms and adaptations are tutelage, and their trace lies in apprenticeship.

Indeed, hauntology requires that every moment of claimed change becomes suspect; or, as Derrida phrases it, "Haunting belongs to the structure of every hegemony."[7] Emancipation as a mode of freedom is a hegemony that haunts. It is the persistence of Black life-forms that continually both show up and offer other possible ways of living a life beyond all bounds that makes evident the haunting nature of emancipation as a limit on what freedom might be. Black life-forms always find ways to exceed the boundaries of capital and other forms of containment as a way to imagine, build, and produce conduits that lead to collective self-referential lives.

The Atlantic Ocean. The Mediterranean Sea. The Caribbean Sea. These bodies of water and others mark in significant ways what Black life is, and cannot be. I should not know the word, the name Lampedusa. Why should I? What use would knowing that name mean for me? But I live under and within conditions that require me to know that word, that name. That word, that name, characterizes, reminds, and extends Black suffering, fugitivity, and its attendant realities into my life, even when it should not. But the Black life-form as a global out-of-place life-form requires that I know Lampedusa. That its four syllables animate my tongue. It requires that Lampedusa become a part of my language, my history, my being. I now live in relation to Lampedusa. Lampedusa is me, singular and plural. Lampedusa is blackness. To say Lampedusa is to summon Black life-forms. Lampedusa.

If, in another moment, Black cargoes confined to holds of ships could simultaneously be a liability and a profit, that time is with us still. That is, Black and African peoples as liability and profit have been with us from the inauguration of the European trade in African beings in the fifteenth century to its various official ends (1807, 1808, 1834–38, 1865, and so on) to its present forms in terms of statelessness, mass incarceration, and forms of forced migration and exile from home territories, but also in planned migratory practices like temporary foreign worker programs in the wealthy West. Because of the way in which enslavement and its residues continue to be a foundation of Black life, the problem of Black and African salability remains present with us. How might we think the problem of Black salability as a problem of and for citizenship and the nation-state? In the contemporary moment, the logic of Black movement is that the nation-state and citizenship have failed the Black migrant, and therefore act as a push factor for Black beings to move. That the nation-state as an entity itself has continually failed African and Black people is almost never *the* story we hear.

The nation-state as an entity takes its imprimatur and its practices from the plantation economies and logics that foreclosed Black subjecthood in the first instance. Therefore, the forces propelling movement (poverty, wars, environmental disasters, trade imbalances, coups, etc.) cannot be singularly understood as failure, but rather as having achieved the intended effects of how the organism that is the nation-state conditions the lives of Black people. When we think with Wynter and Hall, Black movement is not a surprise but a logical outcome of forces meant to make Black life impossible beyond the Euro-Western scripts of what life should be (i.e., the modernist logics of human perfectibility and capitalist accomplishment). That Black life-forms exist in excess of such scripts is the relation between the culture of catastrophe, living in the wake, and the hauntological evidence of Black existence.

Africans crossing the Mediterranean are responding to the push factors of the global conditions of colonization that have produced global wealth and death unevenly. But to return to Jemima Pierre, Africans are also responding to sites of whiteness, where the value of life appears to accrue more possibilities when in proximity or in relation to whiteness. Thus, the Africans whom I speak of here are not migrating to other African nations as sites of refuge. This particular African movement to "white places" immediately runs up against the asymmetrical global racial logics and practices wherein blackness is not valued and is read as out-of-place. Thus, the deaths of Africans in the Mediterranean and the continued harassment of Africans in major European cities are not surprises; they are, in fact, the logical outcome of historical and contemporary policies and practices meant to take all life from them and only notice them as life insofar as it is a life that produces wealth for the West. It is precisely at the point of movement that African and Black people exercise their subjecthood while encountering the continued constraints of emancipation. In this instance, the long emancipation marks the Mediterranean as an extension of, rather than a new, Middle Passage (see Glissant on extension), working to put limits on Black movement, casting such movement as illegal, undocumented, *sans papiers*, and so on.[1]

The freedom to leave — which, for example, Haitians have repeatedly exercised — is a cause for alarm. It is a break with emancipation logics because it contravenes the practices put into place by the legal rules of emancipation. Such movement flouts the contemporary rules of migration, which began their formal establishment in slavery and its aftermath. It is of particular note that it is Haitians and not other Caribbeans who make these trips on a large scale. (Cubans have too but for different reasons and with different outcomes.) Haiti as the first Black republic that sought freedom and defeated a European army saw its move toward freedom curtailed in remarkable ways, one of the most important being the payment of compensation to French plantation slaveholding interests. This requirement of indemnity for Haiti just to exist as a sovereign nation, as a potential place of Black freedom, prior to the British and American emancipation proclamations, is one of the clearest demonstrations of the ways that the terms of emancipation require certain forms and practices that actually prohibit freedom. Despite the "capital punishment" exacted on Haiti, it remains a hauntological space for Western notions of freedom. Capital and its circulation are central limits to possible freedom for Black subjecthood globally. By this I mean that in both the Americas and the African continent, capital transformed into debt has been one way to prohibit a movement into freedom. What we must acknowledge here is that the long emancipation is produced by a set of conditions that cannot be divorced from the foundational imposition of Indigenous land theft, the enslavement of Africans, and the development of capitalism. The fishing boat is the new slaver plying the waters of the Mediterranean and the Caribbean Sea. Haitian fishing boats meet their counterpart in those boats leaving the African coast, inaugurating the discontinuous continuity of an ongoing spatialized Middle Passage.

Ships that traverse the seas like cruise ships and fishing boats now bear an indelible link to each other through the logics of slavery. The cruise ships bring wealthy, mostly white Westerners to the sunny, sandy beaches of the formerly enslaved in the Caribbean. The fishing boats take those Black beings marked as the inheritors of the legacy of transatlantic slavery and colonization to their watery deaths, even when they reach land. Again, in noticing such asymmetry, one must contend with the ways in which these laboring ships shape Black life-forms. To notice the ongoing terrible legacy of ships and the role they play in the long emancipation of Black peoples is to notice freedom's horizon. The central concern then becomes, how might we reach freedom and what must be destroyed so that it might occur? The ship remains a force in the lives of Black peoples. The ship remains a signifier of global white supremacy, uneven wealth and Black enslavement, African colonization, and a set of global logics that continually place Black life-forms outside of the category of the human. And with all of that the ship is also a vessel of subject-making for Black people who decide to move.

Slave ship logics shape migratory policies and their practices. Katherine McKittrick argues in "Plantation Futures" that plantation logics and futures shape our present mode of spatial practices of life. I extend that argument here and insist that slave ship logics also shape migratory policies and their practices. In "Plantation Futures," McKittrick locates the historical logic of the plantation as the template for the spatial and, thus, social and cultural organization of contemporary life. The core of her argument is that the plantation is not in the past but continues to animate the present and the future through both spatial and other logics that place Black life in continued servitude, precarity, and ultimately death. We live on plantations; our cities are designed by their logics; our practices and demands in regard to something as banal as the notion of customer service are premised on its logics. Following McKittrick's argument, we collectively inhabit a world across race and region where Black life is still in the grip of transatlantic slave relations, practices, and logics. This grip is another iteration of what I call the long emancipation. Indeed, the upshot of what this means for Black subjects is that settlement is impossible; citizenship is a mirage; and the nation-state is the site of our deepest estrangement and our deaths. We were not meant to survive.

Returning to the idea of the ship as encapsulating slave logics, we see how limits on Black movement mean that global white supremacy still mandates when and how it imagines Black people can move. If blackness moves in support of or to shore up some set of Western ideas, then such movement is legitimate. In the ongoing drive for a post-Enlightenment human perfectibility, we can see how these slave logics of movement still work. Take, for example, the assumption that Black people and Caribbean and African nations are lesser than Euro/"white" nations because of a claim of homophobia in the "Black world." Such a claim opens up a very small space in the West for the gay, lesbian, or trans persons fleeing homo-hatred in the South to move without sanction; but if that movement was simply in order to feed one's family, the slave ship logics of containment of movement take precedence. Nonetheless, because Black subjects refuse the slave ship logics imposed on their movement around the globe, the question of freedom appears in the face of limits as a still urgent one for late neoliberal modernist capitalist states. Such desires for freedom have been, in part, a significant element in the new "defense" processes of the security state. But such defenses have always had blackness in the backdrop.

Let us take, for example, *Situation of Migrants in Transit*, a report of the Office of the United Nations High Commissioner for Human Rights, from 2012–15, on crackdowns in twenty-five European countries concerning those people named by state actors as the undocumented, *sans papiers*, or asylum seekers.[1] The practice of stopping and questioning and requiring proof of belonging, of having legally crossed a border, has a long history. And when such practices are applied to Black or African people, it cannot but recall the slave codes of the Americas and pass laws in the Americas and South Africa. In her work on biometrics and other modes of surveillance in a world shaped by US responses to September 11, 2001, Simone Browne has traced the connections between historical modes of surveilling the enslaved in the Americas and the articulation of contemporary "scientific" forms of surveillance and documentation. In an important essay, "Everybody's Got a Little Light under the Sun: Black Luminosity and the Visual Culture of Surveillance," Browne points to the ways in which the law that forced Black people in colonial New York City to carry lanterns as a sign of "Black legal movement" produced, in turn, a code of luminosity that made Black travel legible as legal. She states:

> I use the term "Black luminosity" to refer to a form of boundary maintenance occurring at the site of the racial body, whether by candlelight, flaming torch or the camera flashbulb that documents the ritualized terror of a lynch mob. Black luminosity, then, is an exercise of panoptic power that belongs to "the realm of the sun, of never ending light; it is the non-material illumination that falls equally on all those on whom it is exercised" (Foucault 2003, p. 77).[2]

Browne and others (Martha Jones and Alondra Nelson are two examples) skillfully show how the past of African and Black enslavement and the accompanying racial gaze are the foundation of current practices.[3] The new technological and biometric present and future modes of being and surveillance on which the contemporary Western nation-state now rests its security are also premised on a slave past.

This slave past produced the contemporary Black body now violently policed globally. The metaphysical and ontological transformation that led to Africans entering the holds of ships and disembarking as Black, as Frank B. Wilderson has argued, unleashed new life-forms on the globe. Indeed, it may be the case that Black life-forms are the only "global citizen form" (if such a position is currently imaginable). That is, Black life-forms are global citizens—belonging to everywhere at once. To make such a claim is to redefine cosmopolitanism and wrench it from the earlier claims of white male triumphant privileged travel and reportage that have accompanied most of the ways that the term gets defined. It is possible to define *cosmopolitanism* anew in order to resituate it as a dreadful outcome of the modes of movement and travel now seized by those Black life-forms for whom it was not initially intended to narrate their movements.

As both Caribbean peoples and African Americans reignite conversations and debates about reparations for slavery, we should notice that other ways of making reparations with the violent past are coming into thought. Any call or desire for a more authentic postslavery and postcolonial moment would also necessarily have to be noncapitalist. Those Black life-forms moving without bounds might be a significant ethical answer to claims of and for reparations. Unfettered Black movement is a strike against empire and global reorder.

Even when Black people are not moving in terms of migration, slave ship logics still apply. Forms and expressions of Black embodiment often result in slave ship logics coming into conflict with Black self expression. For example, a significant articulation of our present–future plantation logic can be seen in the ways that the hoodies, the saggin' pants, and rap music as modes of Black beings' self-expression produced via a survival logic of the Black life-form are then understood to be a dangerous threat because of comportment, attitude, or style. Such plantation logics extend the diagnosis of a Black freedom drive as drapetomania into our present time. If the slave who sought to be free of the plantation suffered an illness (drapetomania) that could often be only cured through their mutilated body/flesh or their death, the logic of contemporary drapetomania writes the "illness" onto the hoodie and sagging pants and into Black youth musical and other expressive choices and culture. Thus, Black states of being in which the Black life-form seeks to deform the very context of post-

Enlightenment modernity, to carve out spaces of life, are used against them, to deny them any reach into European articulations of humanity.

In the same ways that the logic of drapetomania reaches into the present, the police are an extension of the pattyrollers, those white men who were organized to curtail the potentialities of Black life-forms. Indeed, policing and justice systems constitute knowledge forms and an institutionality that are fundamentally based in prohibiting Black life as human life. Returning to Wynter, it is not possible to reorient the Americas as a zone of life without first ending the Americas as a zone of Black death. In the zone of the Americas, institutions, knowledge, practice, and politics—all of which are entangled, and all of which fall short in the face of the Black life-form—require wholesale rethinking and remaking. The undoing of the Americas is necessary to stem Black death—in the Americas and globally.

The very basic terms of social human engagement are shaped by anti-Black logics so deeply embedded in various normativities that they resist intelligibility as modes of thought. Yet we must attempt to think them. As mentioned previously, the idea of freedom cannot be divorced from the idea of what it means to be human. Continuing to follow Sylvia Wynter's insights on the problem of European humanism as conceptually engulfing all of what it means to be human, I argue that the very idea of the human requires rethinking in order for an authentic freedom to emerge for Black people. I repeat: what it means to be human is continually defined against Black people and blackness. The profound consequences of having humanness defined against Black being means that the project of colonialism and the ongoing workings of coloniality have produced for Black people a perverse relationship to the category of the human. Our existence as human beings remains constantly in question and mostly outside the category of *a life*; it is an existence marked as social death. The global anti-Black condition produced in the post-Columbus (1492) era still and again manifests itself in numerous ways that have significantly limited how Black people might lay claim to humanness and therefore how Black people might impact what it means to be human in a post-Columbus world. Nonetheless, social death does not entirely capture the dynamic of life that I have so far attempted to sketch. This is why I contest the Euro-American narrative of the human and insist on the Black life-form.

Antiblackness continually produces Black people as out-of-place in (post)colonial locations and white settler societies with numerous and devastating consequences. Further, what I call a *pure decolonial project* remains impossible as long as attention to the deathly production of antiblackness is not central to future political desires. In the context of North, South, and Central America, decoloniality has been offered as a way out of European subordinations. I want to suggest something about decoloniality in concert with an allusion to Derrida. A *pure decolonial project* is one that works to produce new modes of relational logics and conditions in which the racially structured intimacies that European colonial expansion produced, and that we continue to live, might be refashioned.

It is only by positioning antiblackness as central to the ways that European modernity has cemented its global reign, and only by taking on the predicament of Black social death as the instantiation of modernity's project of unfreedom, that any movements seeking to interrupt and to bring to a conclusion Europe's and the West's horrific global reign can be successful. The only ways that a decolonial project may avoid its own demise are by engaging the conditions of the invention of blackness, how that invention produces the manifold conditions of unfreedom, and how those conditions produce various genres of the human that are continually defined against blackness.

Taking seriously and continuing with Sylvia Wynter's insights in "Unsettling the Coloniality of Being/Power/Truth/Freedom: Towards the Human, after Man, Its Overrepresentation—an Argument" and her claim that the human is always hybrid—that it is *bios* and *logos*—we might begin more carefully to glean how Black people's insistence on their humanness continually alters and changes the "genre of the Human." In the realm of the post-Columbus colonial project and its resulting global "coloniality of being," Black people have been its most phantasmagoric creation.[1] While it is clear that slavery and other forms of captivity existed prior to transatlantic slavery, the particular ways that transatlantic slavery became a central plank of the European colonial project and of its Enlightenment narrative of the human as not a slave is one of the single most important ideological frames of coloniality. It therefore requires careful reconsideration. Christina Snyder suggests in *Slavery in Indian Country* that if we do not adequately understand other forms of captivity (especially as those forms of captivity sometimes promised kinship only to be transformed into chattel slavery), it is impossible to grasp fully the ways in which racial slavery was fundamentally different from other modes of captivity. Consequently, Frank B. Wilderson, working out of an intellectual tradition that recognizes the uniqueness of modern racial slavery, points out:

> But *African*, or more precisely *Blackness*, refers to an individual who is by definition always already void of relationality. Thus modernity marks the emergence of a new ontology because it is an era in which an entire race appears, people who, a priori, that is prior to the con-

tingency of the "transgressive act" (such as losing a war or being convicted of a crime), stand as socially dead in relation to the rest of the world. This, I will argue, is as true for those who were herded onto the slave ships as it is for those who had no knowledge whatsoever of the coffles.[2]

Wilderson narrates Black coming-into-being and thus Black being, and his idea of the "void of relationality" helps us to make sense of the ongoing stability of antiblackness. It is my contention that Black ontology must be central to a radical or new humanism, as Frantz Fanon articulated it, in these times of paradoxical and contradictory planetary human intimacies. Post-Columbus colonial frames for experiencing humanness, and the absence of it for Black people, continue to overdetermine postmodern conversations on what human means. This overdetermination means that the possibilities for creating significant and lasting cross-racial, indeed, cross-human, solidarities seem to remain out of reach. They seem particularly out of reach for those of us who desire to bring to a close the present dreadful duration of Euro-American human organization of life that foundationally excludes Black people. Yet resolving the multiple ways in which anti-Black coloniality frames the human present is central to achieving any possible decolonial future.

Wynter's articulation of the coloniality of being is crucial to engage in relation to contemporary debates on settler colonialism in the Americas. It is precisely in the context of antiblackness that the language of settler colonialism reaches its limits of usefulness and precision. The very invention of Black people as part and parcel of European colonial expansion has aided the practice of settler colonial societies and simultaneously undermined them by producing a new kind of indigeneity in the West. By this I mean, the invention of Black people troubles understandings of land, place, indigeneity, and belonging because the brutal rupture that produced blackness has severed Black being from all those claims now used to mark resistance to modernity's unequal distribution of its various accumulations. We might have to think indigeneity as a more flexible process of critique and resistance to modernity rather than as an organic identity. Further, I suggest that to invoke indigeneity as an "other" identity is already to accede to Europe's Enlightenment and the modernist anthropological project of categorizing humanness on its terms and logics.

Some contemporary arguments against the ongoing colonization of Indigenous peoples in North America do not adequately sustain a thoroughgoing critique of colonialist capitalism, because such a critique would recognize the nonhuman status of the Black and the ways in which Black people's legacy as a commodity haunts the very status of the human and indigeneity in the capitalist present. Bypassing such an engagement, those arguments and discourses find themselves—even if involuntarily—embedded in anti-Black thought. As commodities of the colonial project, Black people have remained outside modernity's various progressive and/or liberatory reinventions of the human (in terms of gender, sexuality, disability, or trans practices). They have remained overdetermined by racist epistemology. I am not here attempting to produce some kind of competitive oppression exceptionalism. Rather, my aim is to point to the profound ways in which Black being is directly implicated by negation and devaluation (as a negative foil, that is) in the ongoing production of the diversity of what Wynter calls the "genres of Man."[3] Wynter's genres of man mean to have us recognize how Europeans' partial representations of themselves have become the totality of what it means to be man and, of course, human. This conception of the human puts in place genres of man, by which we mean a series of replications of the human (*the black, the red, the yellow*). These typologies then fail to live up to European conceptions of the human as man.

The colonial history that gave rise to contemporary life in the West haunts our present. It is not yet behind us, despite our best desires. Every Attawapiskat, every riot in London, every police shooting in local neighborhoods, every deportation, every dead child in Haiti is the fruit of the violence seeded in collective colonial encounters and their aftermath. The ways in which those diverse but interconnected colonial trajectories continue to frame our relationships to the "happy story" of an egalitarian, democratic West and its unfolding possibilities of assumed rights and identities must continually be called into question. Any social, political, and cultural proximity to the "good life" in the West, still and again, largely depends on our historical relationship to the hierarchical practices of colonial ordering and management and on the ongoing purge of the Black from the category of the human. An administrative system of rule founded on Indigenous genocide, on the making of blackness as social death, and on Black people as the ultimate antihuman others frames our social relations, our intimacies, and it remains the immediate ground of living life in our collective present. Crucial to this ordering and management is the production of what Wynter calls in "On Disenchanting Discourse" "behavior-directing signs": those cultural practices and structures, and that racial ordering, in which Black life is always less valued.[1] Our present, putatively post–civil rights and postcolonial, conditions continue to produce behavior-directing signs (such as NHI, or "no humans involved").

I write from within the geopolitical borders of Canada, and my thinking is influenced by witnessing the Canadian state's production and treatment of forms of being it deems less than human. As a response to those practices, there has recently been a push by conservative Indigenous leaders to align themselves with capitalist neoliberalism instead of seeking a radical intimacy of cross-racial solidarities against colonialism and antiblackness. The political urgency for a radical project of how to live life differently remains unmet. One of the central conceits by which Black people are removed from humanness is that they are constantly situated as out-of-place. This out-of-placeness, especially in relation to poor Black people, has profound life-and-death consequences that become highlighted in the extreme in the carceral states of Brazil and the United States.[2] A Black out-of-placeness is produced and implemented by practices like stop-and-frisk and "carding," measures used disproportionately against young Black people across the North Atlantic zones (New York City, Toronto, London). It is also produced by state practices of deportation and the restriction of labor options for many Black people to imperial armies, prisons, and the informal sector called the drug trade—dangerous and deadly labor, all of it. These are the profound anti-Black conditions of our global past and present.

The oppressive technologies of modern and postmodern capitalism have adapted and renewed themselves in inventive ways, so as to reproduce a global neocoloniality to which there is no outside for anyone. Despite this, there has been a pervasive silence from "ethnic" neoliberals in debates on settler colonialism and on indigeneity's conservative and comprador tendencies.[3] Unremarked upon, for example, are Canada's Indigenous Conservatives (Leona Aglukkaq, parliamentarian in the former Canadian Conservative government; Patrick Brazeau, appointed senator by the former Conservative government) and others: Shawn Atleo (former chief of the Assembly of First Nations, the leading organization that negotiates with the government, who was considered close to the Conservative government) and then Perry Bellegarde, who in their roles in government and extragovernmental organizations have attempted to bypass and ignore the issue of coloniality. Given the ways that Indigenous abjection is shaped by the ongoing colonial project of the Canadian nation-state, the language for considering Indigenous "coloniality of being" in contemporary debates remains, at this time, fairly inchoate. And yet a push for Indigenous capitalism, alongside the attempt to produce continually wasted populations of "nonresourced" Indigenous communities, is an important example of the ongoing adaptability of late-modern capitalism as neoliberal incorporation. Resistances to these practices and incorporations call for relational political logics, if those resistances are to begin to undo that "coloniality of our being(s)." Studies of marginality remain silent on these relations because so much political discourse remains locked in demonstrating our subaltern realities and committed to inclusion in a paradigm of expansion that sits at the core of the colonial and neoliberal capitalist project. Everybody can produce a perverse desire to belong to that which does not guarantee life. This is clear in the way that a significant element of the contemporary debate has shifted to making Indigenous claims that reproduce Euro-centered nativism and express a desire for an iteration of emancipation, the terms of which can only result in continued and new forms of unfreedom for Black people.[4] One of the significant problems of the contemporary debate in and on settler colonialism is the conceptual framework that assumes everyone—individuals and groups—to belong somewhere, to be entitled to, and to desire some kind of original homeland: to have their own place. Such a claim to "homeland" does not work in the context of postenslavement, post-Enlightenment epistemic antiblackness, violent displacement, and the rupture of Black kinship.[5]

A central problematic of imagining new political futures in geopolitical spaces like Canada and the United States is how to think through the complicated challenge of a coloniality that has been maintained within new neoliberal modes of individualism, citizenship, identity, and belonging. These instantiations of late-modern capitalist coloniality work to produce a global space of competition alongside overlapping strategies that continually create disadvantaged and disposable groups, while seducing small numbers of the excluded, all the while keeping in place Euro-American hierarchies that date back to the colonial period. To use an example from the United States, the Cherokee Nation's attempts to de-enroll from the nation the descendants of Black freedmen show one way that coloniality functions to produce a Euro-centered nativism and to produce Black people as continually out-of-place, even in Indigenous contexts. The Black and "mixed-raced" descendants of Cherokee enslaved and freedmen had long held membership in the Cherokee Nation postslavery, until 2007, when a vote was taken to deny them their membership. This "battle" over who is a Cherokee or, put differently, who belongs to the nation, who is in place, and who has claim, highlights the ways in which the asymmetries of contemporary neoliberal economy, politics, and culture work in our time.

In a time when the ongoing colonial intimacy of encounter between Black and Indigenous could have been prized as *a different way of being*, instead it was undermined in an attempt to limit who might benefit from Cherokee resources. That is, the distribution of resources in terms of access and ownership and their concomitant multiple forms of dispossession produce relationships to capital that force, but also allow, white and nonwhite groups to act within the historical legacies of colonial racial ordering, in practices that extend beyond internal Canadian space. One of the shortcomings of scholarship on settler colonialism is the assumption that Canada's colonial practices end at the geographic border of the modern nation-state. The work of Peter James Hudson on the history of Canada's banking system amply demonstrates that Canada's colonial project stretches far beyond the geopolitics of the "entity" we now call Canada.[6] Articulating Canada's role exclusively as a settler-colony in North America does not adequately address its various colonial trajectories. Hudson's work on the Canadian banking system and its exploitation of the Caribbean region reminds us that Canadian colonialism has meant more than the occupation of North American land and territories, more than the management and curtailment of peoples' rights and the exploitation of the land and its resources on the North American continent. To more fully address Canada's role in coloniality, and this includes its reach and practices, discussions of settler colonialism must also entail an understanding of economic, political, and cultural activities which recognizes that Canadian colonial practices far exceed the traditional marker of its historical colonial geography. Canada's engagement in colonial practices in the global realm is distinguished by its role in white capitalist structures and practices that assign value and nonvalue especially to Black and Indigenous peoples.[7]

A number of major Canadian banks (Royal Bank of Canada, Canadian Imperial Bank of Commerce, Bank of Nova Scotia) have long occupied the financial landscape of the so-called archipelago of poverty in the Caribbean basin. These Canadian financial institutions have not sought to service or to invest in the region but rather to extract "resources" back to the nation of Canada. This kind of "overseas" neocolonialism coupled with an "at home" colonial project produces some very complicated conceptual dilemmas for thinking about the culture and politics of coloniality in Canada. That many practices of Canada's colonial project go beyond its geopolitical borders as a nation means that the ways in which different nonwhite bodies are *placed within* and/or *arrive at the borders of* the contemporary Canadian nation-state constitute a complex story of place-making or its denial, of arrival and becoming, or of constantly being made to exist out-of-place.

A critical engagement with coloniality, therefore, demands that we see the mutual imprint of and the overlap between the "reservation," the "housing project," and the "priority neighborhood" (the name given to the archipelagoes of poverty in Toronto), the project of deportation, and the dispossession of people beyond Canada's borders. In each case, the very terminology delineates a specific, if limited, space and an out-of-place-ness for those marked as abject and waste within the boundaries of the nation-state of Canada. Such a range of abjection is possible because of capitalist practices and the constantly flexible dynamics of coloniality, which also produce permanent hierarchical, ranked, ordered positions for the disposable bodies between and across the various sites of capitalism's practice. Progressive scholarly discourses that refuse to acknowledge these leaks remain embedded in the very terms of human life that they seek to overturn.[8] Zainab Amadahy and Bonita Lawrence, for example, write: "From Indigenous perspectives, the true horror of slavery was that it has created generations of 'de-culturalized' Africans, denied knowledge of language, clan, family, and land base, denied even knowledge of who their nations are."[9] This kind of thinking relies on an anthropological discourse of lost origins and fails to comprehend the inventive being of blackness that emerges in the context of the terrible upheavals of slavery, coloniality, and the transshipped.

Critical articulations of settler colonialism need to engage the conditions and ideas of the plantation, the reservation, the ghetto, and neocolonial dispossession, revealing the particular euphemisms of those discursive and violent material constructions, but also their linked and shared realities as the result of the logic and practice of antiblackness and therefore a wider reach of coloniality. Only this *relational logic* can address the project of Canada, which has skillfully produced those sites as *nonrelated entities* with separate dynamics so that "priority neighborhoods" have nothing to do with banlieues and neither of those have anything to do with European colonial practices in Canada's reservations, nor with the economic and cultural interests in the Caribbean. Against this logic, which reproduces exclusive frames of human value and Black unvalue, we need modes of thinking capacious enough to work through the challenge of Black being that coloniality has configured and employed as its most significant and foundational human project of racist management and order. The Black body is the template of the abjection by which the human was produced. The oppressions and the seductions of capitalism in late postmodernity do not simply replicate colonialism's "Red, White, and Black" brutal past, for after all, a Black man became president of the United States, and in the Canadian nation-state Indigenous peoples participate in statecraft too.[10] One cannot stress enough capitalism's foundation as well as its constant and continuous production of death in which all nonwhite bodies are mastered into a project of disposability.

In Ottawa in 2012, a summit between Indigenous leaders and the Conservative Canadian government took place. This gathering was in part produced by the spectacle of ongoing colonialism at Attawapiskat, and it was compounded by the excesses of coloniality elsewhere.[1] The Conservative government framed the conversation at the meeting as one of providing and assuring the community access to capitalism and its many resources. That this was the government's intention was made clear through the constant refrain of bringing "in" Indigenous peoples. An invitation to participate more fully in capitalism was offered as a form of justice by the colonial state. Participation in colonialist exploitation becomes justice, but only if and when resources in territories or the territories themselves are needed for capitalism's expansion. Former Canadian prime minister Paul Martin set up a foundation called the Martin Family Initiative with support from the banking industry (Scotiabank specifically). Its work is to make sure that First Nations/Indigenous peoples are more intimately tied to contemporary Canadian capitalism. The Martin Family Initiative has an educational program that teaches Indigenous students how to produce business plans among a range of other "skills" meant to alleviate their "outsider" status within the nation. These programs are driven both by Indigenous demographics and by a white desire to secure the future of capitalism by incorporating a previously ignored population into late-modern capitalism by way of the lure of small rewards. However, achieving the kinds of justice Indigenous communities require, in which their forms of life are fully acknowledged, would necessitate not inclusion but significant opposition to capitalism in all its present forms. It would require an alignment of Indigenous claims against ongoing colonial practices with radical Black demands that also require relief from colonialism so that their collective lives can be achieved. What we might call "Black freedom" is only possible in distinct opposition to capitalism, historically and presently. Given that the Black body was an instrument of capital, as well as a significant producer of it—it was both commodity and labor—the question of freedom and capital is a particularly knotty one for Black being. Given the intimate crossing of blackness and capitalism, "Black freedom" as a claim, as a possibility, challenges us to imagine and to produce new modes of life that might be in accord with some of the most radical global Indigenous calls for a different kind of world. It is precisely in the moment that Black being can enjoy full human status (the small *h* for *human* here signals Wynter's concerns for a humanism beyond Euro-American articulations) that we begin to see the possibility of a new world yet to come. I mean here that Black being fully expressed would undo the brutal effects of Euro-American articulation of the human and thus inaugurate a different world, that new indigenisms enter the world.

I reiterate here that engaging the epistemological formations of antiblackness is not and cannot be merely one mode of thought among others. Thinking through antiblackness gives and activates a lens to see the human radically differently, to see that its present incarnation has been contingent on the production of other beings' unhumanness and unfreedom. It is, in fact, only by engaging antiblackness as a foundational limit to our collective livability that the overarching racial capitalist ordering of neocolonial peoples, Indigenous peoples, and Black peoples are made visible. The site of liberalism's compromise, by the induction and seduction of selected Black and Indigenous individuals and/or groups, only shores up, as a complementary feature to violent intrusion, the production of disposability.

At this late stage of capitalist modernity, the Canadian nation-state's flexible conceptions of sovereignty, nation, and self-determination are meant to ensure capitalist longevity, secured through incorporation. In the case of Attawapiskat and other places, no such flexibility is evident in the face of an absence of desirable resources. Attawapiskat is an interesting case here for many reasons. It is a territory lacking in natural resources in the places where people live but resource rich in the immediate surroundings. Where the people live is a site that is not needed for the transportation of resources, and so its appeals to the national government for economic resources are dismissed and treated with disdain. This disdain is, for me, the evidence that, regardless of racial history, those territories that possess the resources (in this instance diamonds) to continue to aid in the production of capital are able to find a place in the late capitalist modern nation. Those without resources cannot. My point here is that capitalism continually modifies and "includes" formerly denigrated others on its own terms and gives way to previously excluded people if those people can now fuel its engines. Attawapiskat cannot fuel capital's engines, and therefore it must be managed. Radical discourses and practices that seek to overcome coloniality might want to refuse the logics of belonging to place, in the sense of past ownership of or claim to land, and instead forge a relational logic with Fanon's landless "damned of the earth."[2] Such a claim is not to ignore that human beings need to belong; rather, it is to position belonging outside its historical, naturalized, quasi-organic trajectory and to create another form of sociability not premised on a history of racist social, political, and cultural gradations and exclusion.

The ongoing disposability of Black bodies in Canadian society has created Black severance and, as a consequence, estrangement from the geopolitics of nationhood, no matter how broadly or inclusively defined nation might appear to be in the multicultural Canadian sense. We can conceive of anti-Black racism as the crucially important element of the production of nationalist coloniality in which the Black subject is never able to occupy the site of incorporation into the nation-state because blackness was deemed as fundamentally disjunct with the idea of a nation of free subjects. The fundamental out-of-placeness for Black bodies persists, even if ambivalently attenuated by partial inductions into late capitalism as it seeks new bodies in its constant crises. But the more fulsome social reality is that those inductions of the select few do not by any means outweigh the social, cultural, and political expulsions on a mass scale.

What I earlier referred to as a *pure decolonial project* gives up the politics of organic "identity" in favor of a mobile "politics of thought." This "politics of thought" will be able to critique coloniality's most profound epistemic operations, which have produced knowledges of bodies "in place" and "out-of-place" and the economic and material practices that have resulted in death-worlds for Black people. To acknowledge these death-worlds is an urgency: from that radical vantage point, it becomes possible to conceive of forms of relationality and intimacy, of new modes of humanness beyond capitalist (post)modernity. In a postcommunist world, and a neoliberal globe, thinking, articulating, and moving toward different and new modes of human life is our present challenge. These new modes call for moving beyond and against the "happy story" of progressive liberation of indigeneity in the "native land," against the illusion of a move into the bounty of rights and freedoms. To refuse such a "happy story" is to account for the ways in which history might offer us a better calculation of how to alter the human yet again in our time.[3] Such an alternative will require the production of "new indigenisms" of our globe, and those new indigenisms will require of us conversations, debates, politics, and policies that are centered in the "catastrophic culture" that has brought us together. Edward Kamau Brathwaite, in his lecture "Middle Passages," articulates what he calls "the literature of catastrophe" as the by-product of European colonial expansion.[4] Brathwaite points out that this catastrophe of colonialism produces death, racism, environmental degradation, and so on, but it also produced jazz; Caribbean, African American, and Indigenous literatures; and other cultural forms and practices that have reshaped the globe and human life. I adapt his term to articulate a *culture of catastrophe*, which draws on his insights. Such a catastrophe has the potential, however, to shape profound human possibilities and potentialities. A *pure decolonial project* works the ruins of catastrophe to shape an "other" human intimacy based on the "politics of thought" and thus on mobile association, not on preordained belongings to place and graduated identities.

16. FUNK: A BLACK NOTE ON THE HUMAN

The colonized man who writes for his people ought to use the past with the intention of opening the future, as an invitation to action and a basis for hope. But to ensure that hope and to give it form, he must take part in action and throw himself body and soul into the national struggle.
—FRANTZ FANON, *The Wretched of the Earth* (1963)

Per Harold Cruse I believe there may be remedial and revolutionary implications to black cultural nationalism considered as a political strategy. These derive from black culture's proven capacity to re-invent capitalism's cannibalization and commodification of revolutionary ideas. By necessity our radical aesthetic tendencies have evolved within a context where commercial exploitation and excommunication from the mainstream went hand in hand.
—GREG TATE, *Flyboy in the Buttermilk* (2015)

Nevertheless, Gaye's work, regardless of its lyrical surfaces, in its blurring of the lines separating sex and formal politics, public and private, and the sacred and the profane and its characteristic multiple and often ecstatic vocalizations, would center on one basic concern: the location and character of substantive emancipation.
—RICHARD ITON, *In Search of the Black Fantastic* (2008)

I had a couple of times onstage when I really felt free.
—NINA SIMONE, in *What Happened, Miss Simone?* (2015)

Meditating on funk is a mode of expressive thought. I grew up in the 1970s with two very distinct meanings of funk. First is *funky*, as in body odor, and second is *funk*, as in seriously danceable music. Those two notions of funk always met at the junction of the word *bad*. Either one smelled "bad," meaning nasty, or one was a "bad" dancer, meaning you could funk, you could get down. From the "funky chicken" to "kung fu fighting" to "everybody get up to get down," funk was, and is, always a call to some kind of action. *Funk is impulse, funk is soul, funk is Black, funk is queer, funk is . . .*

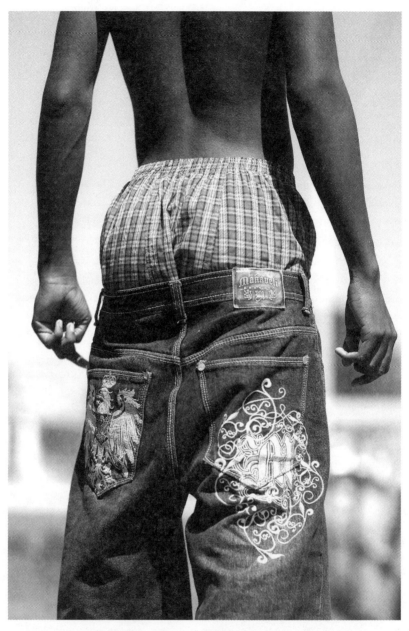

FIGURE 16.1. Saggin' pants model, 2009. Photo by Joe Raedle; courtesy of Getty Images.

In this narrative of funk that I am offering, funk is both bodily and something more. The something more is style and attitude most often represented in forms of dress, comportment, language, sound, and music. In funk, we see Black people take hold of their bodies in ways that demonstrate a sense of autonomy and self-creation beyond the imposed scripts of what a Black life should be. In this way, funk refuses the too-easy script of death demonstrated in its multiple expressive modes of forms of Black life beyond white supremacist logics.

The long and now well-developed debates and dialogues about what constitutes freedom in Euro-American philosophy cannot offer us a way to adequately make sense of the funkiness of Black life. In this work, I refuse engaging that history of thought as a route toward thinking what Black freedom might be, how it might be analyzed, and how we might even notice its possibilities. Since that body of work has either been silent on or elided the history of Black unfreedom, even as Black unfreedom haunts its own conceptualization of freedom, I seek to do something different by resisting engaging it as a way to uncover that on which it remains continually silent. Funk is a prime example of the way in which Black life deconstructs the limits of Euro-American modernist humanism.

Here I move from the fantastical to the ordinary, where the ordinary becomes fantastical. The doubled meaning of fantastical, I argue, is the space where Black freedom might be glimpsed, if not achieved. By this I mean that Black life and its expressions require us to think in ways that both inhabit and simultaneously refuse the normative articulation of what it means to be human in a late-modern capitalist world. Indeed, funk's evidence provides us an opportunity to rethink normativity in a manner that allows us to clearly see the limits of contemporary humanism.

Richard Iton's insistence in *In Search of the Black Fantastic* that "blackness is a constitutively modern albeit unstable formation (i.e., its commitments to possibilities in excess of and beyond modernity)" is crucial for understanding the manner in which blackness is entirely modern and simultaneously beyond and in revolt against the modern.[1] It is precisely this complication of how the modern works in and on blackness and how blackness works in and on the modern that I attempt to come to terms with in these pages. Central to this concern is the invention of the Euro-American human as a category that the Black life-form can only fail at in any attempt to inhabit.

The human as we know it and experience it is a fairly recent invention, less than five hundred years old, and it was forged in the context of the encounters of post-Columbus, European colonial global expansion. Whenever the human is invoked, we are simultaneously invoking antiblackness and Black unhumanness. Black people just can't be human in the present conception of the globe; we are not subhuman or partially human either—we are another life-form altogether. It is precisely because colonial conquest, resettlement, and death shape our contemporary historicity and praxeology of the human that our scholarly, intellectual, artistic, and activist pursuits must recognize the depth of anti-Black logics and knowledge within them. It is my contention that the ethical question of the human should be: Who wants to be human anyway?

Indeed, the manner in which the European Enlightenment and "modernity/coloniality" has continually defined the human as a mode of various accomplishments or as practices of linear progress, continually moving toward some unspecified mode of perfection, and how that sets in place the conditions for a pedagogy of failure to become a praxis of human life for Black people is everywhere clear. I argue that our inability to think clearly and concisely about the invention of Black people in the Americas remains one of the central political shortcomings of much of our artistic/ intellectual and activist conversations. Indeed, it is not too much to claim that the trajectory of much contemporary thinking has as its "dark side" the ultimate genocide of the Black life-form. What these days passes for radical critique, some of it as affecting a decolonial politics, is always already too tightly bound up with the Euro-American notion of the possibility of perfecting some kinds of humanness. As a consequence, such forms of radicality might be in collusion with the very thing they seek to critique.

In part, my argument is that where the Black life-form encounters Euro-American practices of the human, that Black life-form is the example writ large of the praxis and pedagogy of failure of the modern/colonial perfection of the human. This is not to say that the Black life-form is a failed life-form but rather that Euro-American modernity produces the conditions under which the Black life-form cannot be taken as human life or ever fully human life. It is precisely my argument, then, that the Black life-form in its most radical *livability* seeks to reject and rethink the human as a category through which *pure radical possibilities* for life-making might be available for all of us.

Therefore, I make several assumptions: (1) What it means to be human is continually defined against Black people and blackness. (2) The very basic terms of human engagement, those of the social and cultural, are shaped by anti-Black logics so deeply embedded in various normativities that they resist intelligibility as modes of thought, and yet we must attempt to think them again and again. (3) The profound consequences of having humanness defined against the Black life-form mean that the project of colonialism and the ongoing workings of coloniality have produced for "the Black" (as a type) a perverse relationship with the category of the human in which our existence as human beings remains constantly in question and mostly outside the category of life; our life is *a life* often marked as social death. Thus, global anti-Black conditions are most profoundly produced in the post-Columbus era, which is the same era that gave us our concept and practice of what it means to be human. Those conditions manifest themselves in numerous ways that tend to produce significant limits on how Black peoples might lay claim to humanness and therefore how Black peoples might alter and, indeed, continually change what it means to be human in a post-Columbus world—when and if we assert membership in the category as we sometimes want to do and do.

The question of the human, then, is not settled. And I intend to further unsettle the human through the lens of Black being, as a way to open a terrain for thinking about how life might be differently felt and lived in a social and cultural architecture that post-1960s politics have often sought to renovate and not demolish or transform. Thinking with Wynter and Fanon, as well as with funk masters (Parliament-Funkadelic, Sun Ra, Betty Davis, Millie Jackson, Richard Roundtree, and Pam Grier), my argument is informed by a critique that makes explicit that our activism and "our studies" of the post-1960s era (women's studies, Black studies, gay and lesbian studies, disability studies, trans studies, etc.) have sought inclusion in a system that is fundamentally founded on exclusion and violence, rather than on a desire to radically rethink the possible modes of living a life in a system of relations that we need but cannot yet imagine. Put another way, we have become stuck in our various forms of modern/colonial otherness, reveling in identity recognition and niche access to capitalism and its various institutions while legitimating a world system that is not meant to give many of us life.

Black being, the Black life-form, might be a mode of existence through which, if the intellectual and scholarly apparatus was not fundamentally and significantly in opposition to and in disbelief of Black being and life, Black subjectivity might provide much-needed insight into why Euro-American narratives of the human are fundamentally shrouded in failure for most of us. To be human in those narratives is to desire perfectibility, and therefore many of us sit brutally outside the human form. We are simply not imaginable as perfectible, given our always already narratively damned status as nonhuman life-forms. Really grappling with the nonhuman life-form as a serious intellectual endeavor holds the promise for reinventing the human as something much more than the failed Euro-American narrative. Furthermore, the Black life-form provides us a crucial lens through which to engage analytics of thought that provide more nuanced assessments of the social and cultural architectures created for the singular expression of Euro-American life that can only recognize itself as life itself.

I understand our present conceptions of the human to be founded in the dreadful production of the colonial world conceived in the trajectory of Columbus's voyages to the Americas; the colonization and near genocide of Indigenous peoples and, importantly, their survival; the transatlantic slave trade and its invention and production of Black life; and its aftermath as a constant and consistent antiblackness. Postslavery antiblackness continues to deepen as liberal democratic capitalism appears inevitable and a piecemeal politics of intervention is offered up as radical. The long emancipation, like the afterlife of slavery, is the full social and cultural architecture that has maintained as its foundation the racial ordering of human life in which only certain lives matter and are even considered *a life* as the unfolding of Euro-American dominance has articulated itself globally. It is precisely by acknowledging that the human as presently lived and experienced takes it imprimatur from such a history that we might do more than merely oppose it, or renovate it, but rather seek to articulate new modes of living life that banish Euro-American present orders of the human. To be able to achieve such a desired result that is conceptual and political is to ask that our art and activism do more than seek refuge in the structures as they presently exist, given those structures are foundationally about producing an unequal world and making some life-forms unlivable. Indeed, New World Black subjectivity in its most radical articulation requires that we imagine life anew and beyond the instituted behavior-orienting signs of modern/colonial Euro-American logics.

The invention of New World Black people is an outcome of the coloniality of our being. But that invention also forces upon us new modes of encountering the world or, as Wynter puts it, "a new world view."[1] Before we get to the tired question of new for whom, let me suggest that *newness* is for all of us, but in different and deeply profound ways for some of us. In this regard, New World Black people are an entirely new and invented species, a life-form made up by others and forced simultaneously to invent itself continually in the aftermath of its first invention. It is precisely for this reason that many logics presently posed as radical encounters with the modern/colonial order meet their political limits when they must contend with the subjecthood of New World Black people. Certain terms, such as *settler*, *settler colonialism*, *sovereignty*, *territory*, and *land*, return to us in the present as potential modes for decolonization and show their limits when they must encounter Black life-forms. By which I mean that certain trajectories assumed or embedded in those languages cannot offer a nuanced account of Black life-forms. Indeed, it is these very unthinkable (within those languages) life-forms that have produced a set of road maps for living life differently. The road map metaphor is useful here because one of the central tenets that prohibits a grappling with the knowledge that New World Black people offer is that everywhere one turns there is an attempt to continue the out-of-placeness, as broadly defined as you can, for Black peoples.

Indeed, Black musics are one of those roads that complicate out-of-placeness and Black livability. In my view, funk arrives at a time when the elaboration and the promise of Euro-American human categories made it appear as if freedom could be possible. That is, funk arrived post-1960s as a note on unfreedom, a Black note; it drops a UFO on the identity–freedom nexus that we have been stuck in since the 1960s. By this I mean that funk arrives after civil rights, postindependence, women's rights, and gay and lesbian liberation movements, a time when freedom seemed broadly possible by asserting all kinds of identity claims in efforts to reform the state. Funk turns European modernity inside out, on its head, and calls its claims of rationality and logic not just into question but also into disrepute. Funk is a whole other body of knowledge, and this is why it is not intellectually necessary to route its understanding through European continental philosophy. Funk draws on modernity, and it refuses modernity simultaneously as it becomes the best possible example of the modern and postmodern — articulating Afro-futures that only children of transatlantic slavery could give the planet. Black folks have created in their music imaginary worlds necessary for life here, in the now.

The impulse of funk and about funk is one of emotions, feelings, and intuition. Funk is not intellectual. But that should not be taken to mean that funk is anti-intellectual. Funk is thought itself—pure thought. Funk is resonance. Funk is the impulse and the pulse of New World Black people; funk is the alien creation of Europe's slave ships made by Black "transshipped" beings/cultures who were made BLACK in smelly dark holes. New World blackness is conceived in smell. Sun Ra was an alien. Lee "Scratch" Perry is and remains a human computer. George Clinton and Bootsy Collins are Afronauts. James Brown and Rick James were/are monsters. Bob Marley was a living god. Michael Jackson and Prince were cyborgs, whole new humans altogether. Goldie, A Guy Called Gerald, Derrick May, are a po(st)-mo(dern) street gang. Betty Davis, Millie Jackson, Sylvester, June Tyson, Labelle, Mavis Staples, and Martha Wash are Afro-futurists. All of them are funk, and all of them turned European modernity inside out, and in the process the impulse is an ethical and soulful accounting of the human condition pieced together from a "vicious modernism" and a Black self-love. Again, funk is pure thought brought to us by those whose experiences are still understood as alien expressions in a world made by them but launched against them.

Funk is a definition of love that we can't do without. Funk is not love; funk is the practice of love. When you are in the funk, you are working love. Funk as work, as love, as energetic lovemaking produces lovely-smelling bad body odor. If you smell funky, that is a laboring Black body, with its history of smell, both during and after slavery. The funky smells of laboring Black people exude a dignity, a strength, and a power resisting a coming staleness often marked as their deaths.

As Toni Morrison puts it:

The dreadful funkiness of passion, the funkiness of nature, the funkiness of the wide range of human emotions.

Wherever it erupts, this Funk, they wipe it away; where it crusts, they dissolve it; wherever it drips, flowers, or clings, they find it and fight it until it dies.[2]

The most dominant meaning of funk, though, is the music. Funk music is that rhythmic drive that makes you feel the body and lose it all at the same time. Sun Ra, from the "Angel Race" of Saturn, announced he was an alien from outer space. Lee "Scratch" Perry, a human computer, is the inventor of dub in Jamaica. George Clinton and Bootsy Collins are the Afronauts, collectively known as P-Funk, of Parliament and Funkadelic or Parliament-Funkadelic—all the same musicians, a collective of sorts. Bob Marley gave us kinky reggae, funky: these musicians landed a UFO on rhythm, in the groove, to produce funk.

The irony of funk and Black techno musics is that they reclaim an enslaved laboring Black body—a machine of the plantation and postplantation to utter a new narrative in which the Black-funky-techno-body labors to allow us a glimpse at a different possible future. Given that funk is pure thought, what funk offers us intellectually is an epistemological break and, as Derrick May once put it, a species jump, allowing us to conceive and to think new life-forms. By species jump, as he puts it in *Last Angel of History*, May means to signal a deep connection between blackness and technology in which new narratives of humanness, that is, new forms of human life, might come into being and are always glimpsed in Black musics, crafted out of the death-life worlds of bodies made nonhuman.[3] These musical-creative-intellectual renderings are brought to us by those whose experiences are still understood as alien expressions in a world partly created by them, but continually launched against them, but who nonetheless keeps "all y'all asses" moving.

To be Black in this world means to fashion an alternate reality within it, to be funky with and in it. The creative genius of Black artists, in particular, is the way in which they piece together the resources of Black death to create and invent Black lives; this is what I have earlier called *deadly living*. Such creativity is an ongoing project that turns normativity on its head, and it is what we might call "a funk ethics." Such an ethics announces to the world, "I know you mean me no good," and then attempts to live with and in that knowledge. Both Amiri Baraka and Houston A. Baker Jr., writing of the blues, have previously given us a way to think about these difficult conjunctures of Black life and death encapsulated in the musical-philosophical imaginations of New World Black people. A funk ethics forces us to simultaneously confront and deny the forces arrayed against the Black life-form that seek to take even the meager sustenance of life away from "The Black"—that classificatory system of modern/colonial logics. As a type of the modern/colonial order, "The Black" is always positioned in regard to its possible extinguishability, even as it is the very type that makes the modern conceivable and possible; even as it is needed.

Let me give another example from the annals of Black music. I recently came across the story of how Charles Mingus would have a pot of soup on the stove in his apartment all day and sometimes simmering for weeks. Apparently, he would add a carrot, some spice, or something else to it as he attempted to get it right—Mingus's soup was always a certain kind of unfinished delicacy aiming for perfection and never reaching it, not wanting to reach it. Similarly, Mingus came to stop referring to his *band* and his *tours* by those terms; he preferred the term *workshop* instead. In Mingus's soup and his insistence that his band and tours were workshops, I find the suggestion of a certain "to come" moment, a radical futurity or utopia that he refused to name, not unlike his funk brothers, but one he nonetheless knew we needed. What was being worked out? Why this desire to produce ongoing unfinished projects, projects that continually required revision? I would suggest that New World Black people play a function of reminding us that much is not yet finished, that life is a constant and unending revision, that conclusions are violent-orienting projects that preempt new forms of human life. The seductions of our moment offer up loose bromides on finished projects, like Obama being a culmination of some kinds of politics, but on closer inspection the trajectory of those bromides is the continued encirclement of Black death-life. Yes, Black death-life. Black people are born in death and must make lives out of it.

I would bravely amend the quotation from Fanon that began the previous section only to assert that in our moment this is a global struggle and not a national one. Capitalism's permanent crises presently being managed through modes of difference in which an expanded Middle Passage from Africa to Europe has firmly announced itself, this time seeks to put into relation the evidences, as in bodies and lives, of the catastrophic reorderings of post-Columbus movements! Our "new" global intimacy requires increasing forms of violence to hold such intimacy at bay, all the while celebrating an anemic global traffic of capital and its elite defenders across nations and nation-states of all kinds.

The remaking of mankind or genres of the human, as Fanon and Wynter, respectively, term what is at stake, a reordering of the globe, in which freedom is possible, requires us time and again to contend with the "race memory" of the Enlightenment and modernity as not just belonging to nonwhite people, and not just a temporal or periodized account (i.e., before and after the Second World War), but as the foundation of a range of practices and ideas that have come to organize all planetary life. The phrase *race memory* is meant to invoke what Hannah Arendt might call "universal responsibility" against the likes of Kenneth Warren's "what was African American literature" and his claim that African American literature had come to an end in the moment of the election of Barack Obama, and instead in solidarity with Nicholas Payton's heuristic articulation of Black American Music (BAM).[4] Payton refuses jazz as a category of music and instead insists on BAM as a way to account for Black music as a part of the deep race and body memories of Black people. Payton is not simply resisting; he is articulating funk. The two radically different positions require a different approach to the logics of community, proprietorship, and universal claims. Arendt writes: "For the idea of humanity, when purged of all sentimentality, has the very serious consequence that in one form or another men must assume responsibility for all crimes committed by men and that all nations share the onus of evil committed by all others."[5] Arendt might appear to be offering a one-size-fits-all model, but I think something else is at stake in her suggestion. An ethical accounting is at stake. It is one in which the mathematics of humanness require a radical recalculation in which only revolution, this time global revolution, revolution beyond nation and nation-state, beyond racial, gendered, and ethnic categories and imaginaries, beyond the category of Man, indeed in revolt against it, can produce the space and time of the freedoms we have not yet achieved but that we desire.

We glimpse such revolt in BAM and/or funk continually, in its unruliness, in its profane utterances, in its refusal of normativities of all sorts, in its funkiness. Take, as an example, *We're New Here*, Gil Scott-Heron and Jamie XX's remixed collaboration of Scott-Heron's final (2010) album, *I'm New Here*, as it announces such possibilities, as the Black man and white boy produce for us BAM, requiring us each to have different relations to sound, song, and body and thus what might be possible in a future time. Since the remix is itself at the very foundation of Black music. (This is one of those futures that could get misread as multiculturalism, but it's not. It is instead an instance of Afro-futures, because the remix is both past and present of Black life.) Or David Bowie's most successful album *Let's Dance*, what I call a *subfunk album*. By that I mean its rhythms are so suffused with funk thought, practice, and even ethics that to call it derivative would not do it justice and would deny its Black foundations. And once one accounts for Nile Rogers's role in the production of the album, and the enduring queer figure of Luther Vandross's background vocals, Bowie's subfunk is infused with meaning and a funk ethic that brings Africa and Atlantic crossings into view. Bowie's personal funk might be said to find its afterlife or reconnective ethic via a sex life with the African model Iman, marking yet again the sexual history that calls forth modernity's coupling as an act of funk's command of our sex lives' historical imprimatur. The mutuality of co-constitution is alive. Funk is the time of revolt and revolution, even if we in the Euro-American West can't seem to act on it. Revolt continually hails us in Black expressive culture. Funk, 'cause another world is possible. A world where we glimpse potential freedom.

He now begins to experience himself through the mediation of stereotyped concepts *specific to a particular point of view* and *visual phenomenology*; in other words, *not* as he is, but as *he must be* for a particular viewpoint.

—SYLVIA WYNTER, "Towards the Sociogenic Principle" (2001)

The transference of white fantasy to black experience, we might say, continues to haunt the black imaginary.

—DAVID MARRIOTT, *On Black Men* (2000)

The Black man's entire body, his deportment, his sartorial expression, his very appearance, and *his inches* always seem to worry. That is, how many inches might be exposed between the waist and the knees, or from the feet upward, to where and how the pants hang. In the late 1990s, I wrote an article for the now-defunct Toronto gay scene magazine *Fab* about the relationship between hip-hop style (?) and (white?) gay male fashion. In that article, I was particularly interested in the ways that practices of both fashion and style required that pant waists be low in order to show off name-brand underwear—a repudiation of an earlier moment of the claim "I don't wear no man's name on my behind," capped off by Marky Mark modeling Calvins for all of us (men) to consume. The erotic style-statement, I argued, brought hip-hop and gay male cultures into closer intimacy than many at the time (1990s) would acknowledge; after all, this was the height of gangsta rap and its supposed homo-hatred. Yet style-politics saw those two cultures in an intimate embrace that they each denied yet also took great pleasure in. Twenty years on, contemporary disciplinary discourse continues to render Black men's style-politics suspect and in the extreme, as a mode of being that sits outside any form of intelligible logics—as funky. Therefore, I propose here a saggin' pants ethics as a way to make sense of this Black men's style-politics.

FIGURE 18.1.
Saggin' pants
prohibition sign.

With this saggin' pants ethics, I offer a new logics of class, creativity, and embodiment that requires that we contend with Black poor men's sartorial choices as an engagement with a larger anti-Black world. LaMonda Horton-Stallings writes, "The stripper, prostitute, video vixen, gold digger, and sexual exhibitionist cannot continue to be the deviant polarity to the working woman, wife, mother, lady and virgin."[1] Though patriarchal imaginaries don't exactly produce the same typology for Black men, following Horton-Stallings I want to suggest that Black poor men and their style-politics cannot be passed off as the alibi for an impossible middle- and upper-class inclusion in an anti-Black world. Indeed, it is not just any saggin' pants that worry us; it is the pants of Black and working-class men that worry us. Black male style-politics (and the inches of cloth below the waist) continually make visible multiple modes of antiblackness. They centralize a politics of things—the things Black people wear and use to make their bodies legible to themselves—and how those things can come to constitute the means by which they are victimized and killed. But I do not rest simply in articulating Black victimization and death; rather, I seek to engage the complicated site of Black things or Black creativity that becomes capitalized and often used against the very Black bodies who invented them in the first instance. While this has a long history, in the contemporary moment and, for my purposes, since the invention and popularity of hip-hop culture in the 1970s, Black men's style, fashion, and attitude have become sites of significant forms of interdiction, violent and otherwise. Black men's style and creative expressive culture linked to the body represent for us modes of potential freedom from which we can glean the workings of an oppressive society in which city ordinances, in particular, have been used to curtail and prohibit these creative expressions and their appearance.

Scott Poulson-Bryant's *Hung* gives us the other side of the inches that in a conversation such as this cannot be ignored—the sexual politics of the Black man's body. Poulson-Bryant attempts to unmake the myth of the big Black dick/penis. His intervention is not a study of the abstracted phallus; it is a study of Black dick/cock and its material, historical, and symbolic resonance, problem, and self-fashioning. Poulson-Bryant's intervention is meant to recall a history of Black racial threat and terror fixated in part on the assumption of the threatening desires of the large and dangerous Black male dick. He writes:

> I think of black-man dick and I think that once upon a time we were hung from trees for being, well, hung. . . . Strung up from trees; lynched to protect the demure pureness of white women; dissed to soothe the memory sin of slave-raping white masters; castrated to save the community from sexual brutality black men trail behind them like a scent—the scent of the stereotypical boogeyman created by the fears of a nation.[2]

Poulson-Bryant—with humor, sensitivity, and sociopolitical detail—demonstrates how the lives that Black men live in North America often do not measure up to the myth of the big Black dick fantasy. Thus, the myth's outsize fantasy is in direct opposition to the sociocultural evidence of Black male everyday life; that is, the big dick is the corollary to small opportunities. But Poulson-Bryant also demonstrates how many Black men seem to also need the myth as a part of their own individual and collective self-fashioning. Thus, the particular and peculiar racial stereotype becomes a crutch through which to engage the larger social context of Black men's displacement on and in other registers of measure(ment) and evaluation in North American society. The "big dick syndrome," as I named it some years ago, is now a fundamental element of the psychic and performative makeup of Black men's individual and collective personalities.[3] In many ways, clothing is an extension of this image economy. Or, as David Marriott puts it, "the black man is, in other words, everything that the wishful-shameful fantasies of culture want him to be, an enigma of the inversion and of hate—and this is our existence as men, as black men"—straight or queer.[4] And when the dick disappears, it goes behind clothing, which takes on our unfreedom, but clothing is not just an extension of the Black male phallus or its replacement. Clothing is a creative and subversive expression of how Black men make lives in the world alongside and with the big dick syndrome.

Clothes and Black male style-politics exist in the gap between self-fashioning that challenges forms of white supremacist comportment and intra-Black heteropatriarchal practices. Indeed, Black men's style-politics articulate and cite other kinds of politics, class positions, gender troubles, and sexual imaginaries to which we should be keenly attuned. I will suspend those other moments to focus on class and its creative energies. Marriott further argues in *On Black Men* that "there is a demand that black men perform a script—become interchangeable with the uncanny, deeply unsettling, projections of culture."[5] It is indeed at the site of culture that Black men's reworking of things becomes hypervisible and criminalized while those things can be simultaneously invisible and unspeakable and at other moments financialized and capitalized and loved.

In *On Black Men*, Marriott returns us to debates about typologies in which he takes up Frederick Douglass, Edward Blyden, Alexander Crummell, and W. E. B. Du Bois and their articulations and desires for Black masculinity. In those debates, the question or notion of imitation is central to what Black masculinity might be in its singular expression. Marriott argues that Crummell understood the Black man's imitation as the ultimate expression of what human civilization might be, and he suggests that Douglass, Blyden, and Du Bois all either argue against Crummell's notion of imitation or are in ambivalent relation to him. I find the history of the debate concerning Black masculine imitation and types useful. Du Bois and his cohort might well be surprised by how Black men are imitated in the twenty-first century. I have previously argued that Black men are offered two types of masculinity: a hard masculinity, assumed to be heterosexual, or its opposite, which is always feminized and rendered *faggot* even when it is not. While these types do not have, as is quite obvious, any empirical reality, they nonetheless continue to frame Black hegemonic masculinities, thereby erasing all the multiple ways in which we, as Black men, express ourselves and practice our being. Indeed, the ways that we inhabit our bodies — through hairstyle, clothes, and other adornments — are central to this typing.

The second half of the twentieth century marked the secure ascendancy of Black popular music as a defining and driving force in the invention and creation of youth culture generally in North America and beyond. By the 1960s, Black popular cultural forms—music, speech, and dress— operated across a racial divide that both cannibalized them and simultaneously attempted to diminish their influence, in a cultural divide that crassly marked rock and roll as white and soul as Black. Black popular cultural forms, however, remained the template for much of postwar popular music and youth culture, even if the cultural arbiters of North American society have denied it. However, all such claims clearly shifted by the 1970s with the ever-increasing dominance of rap music, and its larger context of hip-hop culture, becoming the soundtrack and the attitudinal narrative of commercial and popular culture in the West and globally. Central to these phenomena were and are Black public masculinities and their style, fashion substance, and gesture as defining features of popular cultural expression in the second half of the twentieth century and continuing now well into the twenty-first.

In the wake of such a shift (from denial to proliferation), hip-hop culture and some forms of Black public masculinity have been criticized, banned, and in some cases made illegal.[1] The substance of Black male style has generated enormous intellectual energy, debate, and legislation. Cities and towns have passed ordinances and bylaws on how pants can be worn and how baseball caps should be fitted and where their peak should point. Schools have banned certain kinds of clothing items or ways of wearing them, and heated debates continue about the ways in which prison uniforms and thus prison culture have influenced and continue to influence Black popular culture and thus Black public masculinities.

Following Angela McRobbie's work, it is important to point out that these debates have generally, though not exclusively, followed from "the gendered character of leisure and commercial popular culture" in the late

twentieth century in which men and boys have been the central antago-
nists.[2] Attempting to get an angle or a grip on Black public masculinity is
important work in the context of the ongoing contradictory ways in which
Black men are inserted into and insert themselves into late-modern capitalist cultures. Such insertion occurs both at the level of performance and
articulation and importantly at sites of production and dissemination, in
all of which Black men are deeply implicated.

Richard Sennett has termed the shifts in political economy toward the
end of the twentieth century, which are usually referred to as neoliberalism, "the culture of the new capitalism."[3] In his book that carries the phrase
as its title, Sennett suggests that the changes signal a profound cultural shift
that equals the profound shifts in corporate global remaking. If corporate
global fortunes have no foundational home and thus capital takes flight to
wherever it can best be amassed, he suggests a similar trend exists in the
cultural realm. Sennett maps the trend in relation to the ways in which institutions have been remade so that questions of loyalty and trust are no
longer defining elements of the social compact and a fear of uselessness
becomes a central component of interaction with institutions. He writes:
"The new institutions, as we have seen, are neither smaller nor more democratic; centralized power has instead been reconfigured, power split off
from authority. The institutions inspire only weak loyalty, they diminish
participation and mediation of commands, they breed low levels of informal trust and high levels of anxiety about uselessness."[4] In part my argument is that Black male public masculinities display such anxieties and in
fact might have helped to usher them in. For Black poor and working-class
men, the question of uselessness or usefulness in late capitalism is one lived
in the immediacy of the everyday. As Hartman writes in "The Terrible
Beauty of the Slum," the sociologist is "aroused at the sight of elegantly clad
domestics, janitors, and stevedores; elevator boys in rakish hats preening
on the corner; and aesthetical Negroes content to waste money on extrav-
agance, ornament, and shine."[5] Even their clothing choices point in the direction of this immediacy. By this I mean that one way to read, for example, oversize clothing is to account for what cannot be seen or visualized
by the clothing—a body made useless. Such oversize, or rather outsize,
clothing creates a particular difficulty in assessing body size; in concealment of weapons; in protecting oneself—such clothing is a kind of armor
in unstable times. But such clothing also protects/projects the culture's fantasy of the threatening Black man; fantasy that Black men both play with
and sometimes need for their own protection. There is no easy out from

the contortions in which capitalism has trapped our bodies. While such clothing points to a certain kind of uselessness in terms of questions of decorum and comportment, these clothes are not just a refusal. The clothing choice pushes back and brings into view the now-thin line between the panopticon of the street and the panopticon of the prison-industrial complex, making evident the continuing time of the long emancipation. These forms of interdiction remind and cement for us that Black freedom remains elusive and contested.

Ethically, then, such clothing, like saggin' pants, points to a culture where Black men made useless as labor now mark that uselessness on their bodies. What makes the marking more complex is that it exudes what Ishmael Reed, the novelist, essayist, and playwright, called "black joy." For Reed, Black joy is evident in Black people's aesthetic creative practices from music to literature and everything in between. However, since Black men made useless can still be joyful and such joy is useless to capitalism — that is, Black joy can't be capitalized — anti-Black aggression is what greets it. It is in this light that a *saggin' pants ethics* comes to be. A saggin' pants ethics forces us to contend with the larger culture's anti-Black orientations toward any forms of Black creativity that refuse capitalization. Rap music's mainstream success is fundamentally about its capitalization in a way unmatched by other elements of hip-hop that remain outside hegemonic capital.

Key to this are the ways that some forms of sociological and media studies fail to notice how "ordinary people actually make a small record of their lives through forms of cultural and symbolic embodiment including music, dance and fashion."[6] Black public masculinities use fashion and style to re/design the Black body in an economy that might and does otherwise render that body useless and/or waste. Returning to Sennett, the "specter of uselessness" is one of the principal features of "the culture of the new capitalism."[7] Black public masculinities seek to produce forms of uselessness, like hanging on the block, through complicated and ambivalent gestures that take as central to their expression consumption and, even more important, adornments, gender performances, and bodily markers to reposition their usefulness as a Black life-form.

IN "RECONSTRUCTING MANHOOD; or, The Drag of Black Masculinity," I argued that the neoliberal economy and Black conservative political forces that target working-class and poor masculinities for practicing improper modes of life could not make sense of Black queer and Black transgender peoples who refused to articulate lives as just one or the other thing.[8] In particular, I was interested in pointing out that a Black politics of respectability understands Black poor and working-class peoples as a scourge on Black social and economic advancement and mobility in North America. In that intervention, I sought to bring to the conversation that Black intellectual labor—scholarly and/or artistic—is an urgent labor that requires that we produce new modes of being in excess of those presently presented or on offer. A *saggin' pants ethics* and a *funk ethics* require us to grapple with the ways that Black poor people's creative energies resist being hijacked by capitalization and resist forms of financialization by engaging a practice of uselessness that cannot be cannibalized by capital but nonetheless references Black life as a life worth living in the face of a global system that seeks only to use and/or discard the Black life-form. Black life exists in crevices of the long emancipation, and it is in those spaces that funk erupts, giving us the glimpse of freedoms yet to come.

Instead, the new descriptive statement of the human will call for its archipelago of Human Otherness to be peopled by a new category, one now comprised of the jobless, the homeless, the Poor, the systematically made jobless and criminalized—of the "underdeveloped"—all as the category of the economically damnés (Fanon 1963), rather than, as before, of the politically condemned. With the result that if inside Europe, it will be the Poor who will be made to reoccupy the earlier proscribed interned places of the Leper and the Mad, in the Euro-Americas, it is the freed Negro, together with the Indians interned in reservations, or as peons on haciendas, who will now be interned in the new institution of Poverty/Joblessness.
—SYLVIA WYNTER, "Unsettling the Coloniality of Being/Power/Truth/Freedom" (2003)

Blackness, as we know it, begins in no future. The Black life-form, however, forces the future on us as a nonnegotiable critique of white supremacy and all its post–Middle Passage legacies. The Black life-form, and thus Black studies, calls attention to the limits of the human and freedom as rooted in and routed through forms of thinking and confronting Euro-American knowledge systems of the world that can but display the brutal realities of our now. In part, it is the brutalities that we live—both intellectual and material—that this section seeks to be attentive to in its attempt to grapple with the place of freedom, humanness, and Black studies in the neoliberal contemporary moment.

Thus, it is my argument that the question of the "future of Black studies" might elicit a range of responses depending on one's location. Indeed, if one is located in a US Black studies department, the response might be more sharply animated by a discourse related to funding, faculty lines, and student training than by some other concerns—and this is not to evacuate the critical concern of scholarship, activism, methods, and ethics (the fight at Temple University concerning Anthony Montiero is a case in point).[1] I endeavor to further think through the pedagogical implications of *black studies* (lowercase *b* and *s*) without an institutional name and an institutional location, which is the context that, until very recently, I write from in Canada. This section thinks from a geopolitical location of Black studies outside the United States' institutional knowledge circuit, but nonetheless positioned by that circuit, to attempt to articulate a future for Black studies without a name while recognizing that a name carries with it much that is of political importance.

Through a meditation on the reception of Lawrence Hill's *The Book of Negroes*—which was renamed in the United States, Australia, and New Zealand as *Someone Knows My Name* and translated in the Netherlands as *Het Negerboek*—this section seeks to think noninstitutionalized Black studies. What is at stake in turning to the reception of the novel's title in the Netherlands (where the Dutch version was a direct translation of the original) is how Black freedom might be apprehended in the present world. The debate concerning the changed book title traffics between Black Canada and Black Netherlands, two sites not immediately noticed as sites for Black studies, especially noninstitutional Black studies. Some of the work that noninstitutional Black studies can do is in helping us understand the stakes of ongoing desires for and restrictions on freedom.

In this meditation, I take up Hill's long essay *Dear Sir, I Intend to Burn Your Book: An Anatomy of a Book Burning*, in which Hill responds to Afro-Dutch critics who objected to the book's title *Het Negerboek* and who threatened to burn the book. The renaming of *The Book of Negroes* began in the United States because Hill's publisher there claimed that presale orders were almost nonexistent due to the original title containing the word *Negroes*. In the Netherlands, the book cover was burned because the word *Negerboek* appeared in the title, provoking an international response. I want to query here what travels as Black studies globally by mapping the change (or not) in a title and the controversies around it. How does Black studies name its present and its future, and what is at stake for Black lifeforms in the context of a Black studies and its resultant products that appear to travel only as texts? Can we have a Black studies without a name? In other words, what is the future of a North American and global Black studies project that eschews naming in favor of a political project that arrests and dismantles forms of antiblackness that seek to wrestle away from peoples, now named Black, forms of intellectual sovereignty that might radically transform what it means to live a life moving toward something else in the still-brutal intimacies of a postslavery world?

I still vividly recall the report on the CBC *Evening News at Six* (June 15, 2011) on an event scheduled to occur in Oosterpark, Amsterdam: a planned book burning of *Het Negerboek*. Hill responded to this provocation, which he had received by email from Roy Groenberg, with *Dear Sir, I Intend to Burn Your Book*, using the email's subject line as his title. In the essay, Hill comes to terms with the intention to burn his book and works out his relationship with such acts of censorship. But Hill seeks to do more than cast the event as merely one of censorship; he seeks to make some kind of relationship with his provocateur, thus transforming him into more of an interlocutor. Hill's response to the potential book burning aims to make sense of why the reception of his book based on its title might have triggered such a response in the first instance. But the essay is also a reflection on Hill's work in anticensorship circles in Canada and his work as someone who is an articulator of an antiracist and socially just world.

The Book of Negroes was first published in Canada in 2007 and has reportedly sold more than 600,000 copies there (where a book that sells about 5,000 copies a week is apparently considered a best seller). Hill has won a number of major awards for the novel (including the Commonwealth Prize), and the book has been widely celebrated as telling an important story and also crucially pointing readers to the actual history from which the novel draws its material. I have had conversations with people who insist that every child in Canadian schools should have a copy of the book assigned as a part of their curriculum. This is one demonstration of how precious the tale the book tells has come to be to some people. The enormous popularity of the book on Canadian soil is evident through its sales, its adaptation into a CBC TV/BET miniseries, and especially in the aftermath of the popular CBC book competition Canada Reads. In fact, the popularity of the book and its ubiquity make the controversy around its title in the Netherlands an interesting intervention on why similar concerns or questions were not raised in the Canadian context, given the book's far-reaching impact there.

In the aftermath of the Netherlands story, one begins to wonder what kinds of conversations Hill had with his Canadian publisher about the novel's title. Did he and his publisher simply assume that Canadians would have no problem with the title? Did they discuss the transposition of the actual *Book of Negroes* title of the eighteenth-century record of enslaved people to the novel of the twenty-first century as just adding another layer of authenticity onto the novel? Did they think about whether Black Canadians might have been offended by the title? From Hill's essay at least, it does not appear that he or his Canadian publisher asked any of these questions. For me, that might be the most interestingly untold part of this story—was there any consternation about the book's title from its Canadian publisher? These questions are conditioned by the nonplace of Black studies in Canada as an institutionally recognized formation. Indeed, Black studies in Canada has no name—nobody knows its name.

This is one context in which it becomes quite interesting that the US publisher found the novel's title a problem. Hill reports in his essay that although the US publisher did not find the title offensive, it was concerned that the title would adversely affect sales. Hill writes that with little time to think through the problem of the title, he changed it to *Someone Knows My Name* for US publication. It is the question of sales that might be the most disappointing aspect of this entire sordid episode of a book-cover burning and an aborted book burning in Amsterdam. Of course, publishers publish books to make money and writers write for their living, so the question of book sales is germane to both. But I suggest that Hill's quick fall for his US publisher's concerns about sales given the book's title reveals much about this story. What do sales have to do with good art? What do insult and injury have to do with good art? And if the title of the book held important historical, social, cultural, artistic, and indeed ethical meaning, why change the name for sales? Would readers not eventually find this important story regardless of initial sales? What role would critics and reviewers play in explaining the title? It is precisely at this point that a larger set of questions about the culture industries make themselves present concerning this event in our neoliberal times. If changing the title had more to do with sales than with the artistic, cultural, and political impact of the title and the kinds of conversations and thus learning the original title could and might entail, why change it? While Hill does not fully address these kinds of questions in the essay, it becomes clear that the full financialization of life dictated much that occurred in this incident.

Hill's essay is rooted in a long tradition of correctly reminding readers about the multiple pitfalls of book censorship. But Hill is historically minded and thoughtful enough to know that anticensorship arguments are also deployed against the historically oppressed. Thus, Hill produces the ethical dilemmas of racist literature as a backdrop to working out how he comes to his positions on anticensorship. By recounting his family's very active involvement in civil rights movements in the United States and

Canada, Hill plots the quagmire of censorship in smart, sentimental, and ultimately ethically difficult terrain. Indeed, it is the civil rights family narrative (his father, Daniel Hill, from Missouri, the first director of the Ontario Human Rights Commission, sociologist, historian, and author; and his brother, singer-songwriter Dan Hill of the hit "Sometimes When We Touch") that makes Hill's position on censorship a difficult and nuanced one. He is forced to work out a thoughtful relationship to literature meant to demean and harm, alongside a position that does not call for such literature's banning, but rather for its vigorous intellectual and political engagement. Hill had been a part of such debates prior to his own encounter with his Amsterdam interlocutor, Roy Groenberg. Given Hill's thoughtfulness, it is surprising that in his essay he does not meditate on the relationship between titles and sales.

However, if the change of title was initially facilitated by sales, then, of course the email from Amsterdam is one that can only be surprising. The email from Amsterdam is less interested in the art of the novel, or for that matter the sales of the novel or even the story of the novel, than it is interested in what the title signifies about un/reconciled histories of Black people's enslavement and the still-lingering evidence of such histories in the Netherlands and beyond. Similarly, in the United States, the original title spoke back too clearly to the un/reconciled histories of slavery and postslavery life there. The desire to burn the book is framed through the unreconciled histories of Dutch involvement in the African slave trade. Oosterpark is freighted with symbolic historical significance: the cover burning took place "next to a monument commemorating the victims of Dutch slavery."[2] This is a war of symbols between the author, the publisher, and the Dutch Black objector, Roy Groenberg. It is important to say that Groenberg, chair of the Foundation Honor and Restore Victims of Slavery in Suriname, was not just speaking for himself. The admirable aspect of Hill's essay is his attempt to complicate his response to Groenberg's provocation by thinking seriously about the desire to burn the book and the ways in which he and Groenberg might agree on a number of issues pertaining to postslavery Black life in the Netherlands and globally. It is such openness on Hill's part that makes me term Groenberg his interlocutor and not merely his censor.

Since Hill takes seriously Groenberg's intervention, Hill is forced to work out why such a response to his book might have been possible in the first instance. Despite his staunch anticensorship beliefs, Hill must wrestle with and does wrestle with the fact that the Dutch, like white Canada, have sought to downplay if not attempt to make disappear altogether their role in transatlantic slavery. These respective roles are one of the central considerations in the conversation between Groenberg and Hill. Canada's relationship to and its benefits from transatlantic slavery are so submerged in the national consciousness that raising its specter almost always seems in bad taste. For the Dutch, it is the same, but with overseas colonies and a figure like Zwarte Piet, the Christmas "dark-face" figure who scares bad children, the Dutch's deep involvement in one of the most horrific abuses of human history rears its head at least once a year, not to mention the many formerly colonized arriving at the doors of the "motherland" still and repeatedly.

Hill declares an intimate and ongoing commitment to the Netherlands and Canada. He recounts his many trips and importantly his first trip to the Netherlands as a young man. Thus, he claims to be even more emotionally affected by Groenberg's intervention and to experience it as a surprise given that he (Hill) believes conversation and debate would be more suited to the national temperaments of both places. But it is indeed the tangled and unresolved histories of slavery and contemporary anti-Black racism that complicate how texts are received, valued, and understood to be representative or not of various communities. It is precisely because Hill's novel entered into a field where contestation over a very few or a limited set of Black representations are available that, in my view, it elicited such a response in the Netherlands.

Resorting to having to burn a book as a form of protest tells us something about Groenberg and Foundation Honor and Restore Victims of Slavery in Suriname's access to being heard in other contexts. My reading is not to say that book burning is fine, but rather to point to the different ways in which Black communities have access to intervening in the public sphere and having their views accorded some space for consideration. In the Netherlands, from the persistence of Zwarte Piet, to a magazine's reference to pop star Rihanna as a "nigger bitch," to Black people being beaten up and arrested for protesting Zwarte Piet, the field of Black or rather anti-Black representation is one that is already saturated with negativity.[3] It seems safe to venture the guess that, much as in Canada, the Dutch publisher would not have given any thought to how Black and other nonwhite Dutch people might have responded to the title when acquiring the rights to publish the book. In such cases, do writers also have to think through these minefields for themselves? By taking Groenberg seriously, Hill begins to approach such a question, though he never dares to ask it or attempt to answer it.

Seeing the words *Het Negerboek* on the page as a non-Dutch reader and speaker, but as someone who has lived all my life in the zone of the Americas, the first association I make with it visually is to the word *nigger*. To my eyes, there is something in those letters that speaks of a history of concealment of the ways in which language has been central, if not foundational, to the unmaking of Black people's humanness. Unlike Roy Groenberg, I believe such words must remain with us, not buried, because those words act as reminders of the terrible things that have been done and continue to be done to Black people. Even when the words have been banished, the ideas behind them do still get a Trayvon Martin shot to death. This is why I have come to use the term *global niggerdom* as a way to signal the ways that forms of global antiblackness now circulate from one nation to another: in how poor Black people are housed and policed, what kind of employment (if any) they have access to, and so on. The conditions of the long emancipation are the conditions of *global niggerdom*. Different countries, same conditions for those marked by and inhabiting blackness. Groenberg's protest of Hill's title is, I believe, framed by the concerns and the conditions that I mark as the long emancipation.

Hill's response in *Dear Sir, I Intend to Burn Your Book* opens more questions for me than it resolves. Once routed back to Canada, one begins to ask questions such as: Do Canadian publishers even imagine a Black reading public the way that the US publishers might or did? Are Canadian publishers too steeped in the myths of a Canada that is not troubled by the legacy of transatlantic slavery to imagine such a reading public? What kinds of conversations are editors, publishers, and book marketers having with their writers around these kinds of concerns in the Canadian marketplace? Are there any people working at such levels in the Canadian publishing industry who understand and have the expertise and professional respect to raise these questions? Finally, again, why did Black Canadians not respond similarly to their Dutch kin? Is it that Black Canadians do not think their concerns could be heard? Is it that the Black Canadian success that this novel now represents is so little witnessed that making any noise might seem embarrassing and disrespectful? Again, the issues opened up here are far beyond issues of censorship, as important as that may be. The issues all strike deeply at book publishing in Canada, Black communities, and an imagined reading public that appears not to include Black people as readers too.

I think Hill's *The Book of Negroes* is so well loved because the Black people, as represented by his main character, Aminata, return to Africa, to Freetown, Sierra Leone. The nineteenth-century colonization project is fulfilled with its fantasy of returning Black people to Africa, thereby solving the problem of what is seen as Black unbelonging in this part of the world. As the novel concludes, Aminata returns to England to give an account of her life in order to aid in the abolition of the slave trade—yet another moment of the long emancipation in which the desire for freedom becomes a sensation of our freedom. As Lupe Fiasco reminds us: "Freedom ain't free, especially 'round my way."[4]

We are living in the long emancipation. Since 1834, when Britain "freed" the Black enslaved and they walked off the plantations refusing apprenticeship, freedom has been free-Doom, as Gil Scott-Heron and Kanye West remind us. The actions of those postslave subjects set into motion other movements of people known by the shorthand word *indenture* that further solidify antiblackness as a mode of global behavior. The most powerful impact of the curtailment of Black freedom in the postemancipation Americas—whether revolutionary Haiti, the Anglo-Caribbean, the Francophone Caribbean, the United States, Brazil, Cuba, or more broadly Luso-America—has been in the interruption of postslave freedom through practices that forced Black people to simply try to survive. It is Black people's abilities to survive that animate any possibilities for a freedom "yet to come." Black peoples retain modes of knowledge and being that we might call the future. Without Black freedom, the conceptualization and possibility of a future-to-come do not exist.

Throughout these pages I have invoked the Anglo-Caribbean to signal the similarities across the zone of the Americas in which Black people's desires to be free run up against the limits of emancipation. As I have already outlined, emancipation was not meant to free Black people—the evidence across the Americas is the same everywhere—but rather to place them in a subordinate labor–cum–lack-of-human–cum–condition of deprivation, degradation, and bare(ly) (a) life. Black people's continual refusal of such a condition has resulted in what I have been calling the long emancipation, which is the interruption of post-Enlightenment modernist freedom as it was about to be remade whole cloth by the formerly enslaved throughout the Americas. It is my claim that had emancipation turned into actual freedom, the globe would be a radically different place now.

The history of the blockade of Haiti and its aftereffects; of segregation in the United States; of the denial of racial slavery in Canada; of colonization in the Anglophone and Francophone Caribbean; of segregation in Brazil; and of Cuba (including the ongoing blockade of Cuba, which was slowly being lifted by the United States under President Obama and became unclear under President Trump's leadership) and Latin and South America (the disappearance of the Argentinian Black community at the beginning of the twentieth century) provide abundant evidence that similar practices and modes of behavior arose to preempt the possibilities of Black freedom across the Americas. The legacies of these interruptions remain with us in the contemporary moment, as witnessed in the vicious evictions in 2011–12 of the Black poor in Brazil from their sites of residence for the World Cup and the Olympics—this in order to model a particular kind of modernity, one in which Black displacement always seems to be at its foundation. *Global niggerdom*, the historical and contemporary conditions of slave life and its aftereffects of violence, poverty, brutality, terror, and degradation, continues to be the basis on which all Black people are encountered and made knowable globally.

To repeat, in the contemporary neoliberal moment, we experience what I call *sensations of freedom*. These sensations of freedom are enjoyed and on display in a variety of ways—from the election of an African American president in the United States, to claims of postcolonial conditions elsewhere in the Americas and Africa, to minor forms of visibility politics (televisual and cinematic representativeness) across a range of platforms and institutions. The media and universities have been especially complicit and implicated in the production of such corporate multiculturalisms. Corporate multiculturalism has come to stand in as freedom in a system that cannot produce actual freedom for the Black life-form. Indeed, this sensation of freedom is a significant aspect of the long emancipation. These sensations of freedom are the ruse that neoliberal formations, in particular the nation-state, can make right and just the violent origins of their founding and foundations. Nothing is further from the truth, especially for Black peoples.

As Sabine Broeck and others have pointed out, modernist ideas of freedom lodged in Lockean notions are deeply tainted. Broeck's engagement with Locke's *Treatises* is an excellent case in point. She works against Lockean conceptions of slavery to reveal the manner in which transatlantic slavery had to be ignored and denied and how a particular knowledge of "the slave" needed to exist so that Lockean conceptions of freedom might take shape and come into being. Significantly, Broeck's argument and intervention through her critique of Locke is that European philosophy and political theory have at their core an idea of slavery as "its very particularly indispensable presence."[1] Indeed, Broeck does not mean a nonracial slavery, as propagated by European intellectual thought, but rather the very particular and specific case of New World African/Black slavery that the collective unconscious of European thought has grappled with, most often through denial, misplacement, and outright suppression. For European thought to advance its own narrative of freedom as a nonracial narrative of freedom, "enslavement" had to be its very foundation, Broeck argues. Such a critique of freedom means that Black forms of life are permanently expelled from post-Enlightenment modernist freedom, because its very foundational logics are framed on Black subjection and the denial of Black forms of life, what Dylan Rodriguez has termed "evisceration."[2]

The poet, novelist, and essayist Dionne Brand comes to similar positions in contending with the problematic of freedom and Black life. From *The Blue Clerk*'s "Verso 32," which concerns itself with Black knowledges:

VERSO 32

Here again we have to turn to Charles Mingus's *Pithecanthropus Erectus*. As I read it there is no way of translating this text yet. Its language rejects a conventional translation, that is, once you attempt to translate it into the sense of a language with vowels and consonants say, that is the sort of language that directs sound in a particular direction as opposed to another—let us say into the direction of known conventional languages that we use to "communicate" with, then you are lost. Or the meaning is lost to you. But why talk of translation. That is not really the point. Unless you feel inadequate to your earlier comparison of Mingus and Plato. Yes, only in conveying the breadth of the work. Translation was the metaphor not the thing. I mean. But is it not music, shouldn't you say someone in that vein? No, *Pithecanthropus* is not music, it is a text of philosophical charge. No periphrasis exists. Its ineffability demands another larynx.

VERSO 32.1

Plato was a slaveholder. I cannot get past this. I am a barbarian. That is the way it is. People say that is the way it was. Yes, that is exactly the way it was.

VERSO 32.2

My ancestral line to John Locke. When he wrote "An Essay Concerning Human Understanding" in 1689 he had already been the Secretary of the Board of Trade and Plantations. No one disputes this. He had, too, investments in the Royal African Company, whose holdings along the Gambia included forts, factories, and military command of West Africa etc. , . . . etc. , . . . No dispute here either. These statements—an essay on human understanding, and the board of trade and plantations—these identifiers can lie beside each other with no discomfort, apparently. But as I said, I am a soft-hearted person. I cannot get past this. All and any interpretative strategies are of no help to me. I am just a lover with a lover's weaknesses, with her manifest of heartaches.[3]

Brand's refusal of translation and of interpretation turns our attention to what is in part the work of Black studies scholarship and politics, to resist the desire of explication *as if such explication can itself produce freedom.* In refusing translation and explication, Black studies requires its interlocutors to think otherwise. Such otherwise thinking is usually greeted with logics of unknowing and claims of untranslatability in the Canada from which I write. Black studies' currently partial noninstitutionality in Canada represents the ongoing dilemma around how freedom might be thought there. The lack of full-fledged Black studies programs in Canada works both to reproduce modes of unfreedom and to simultaneously allow for eruptions of freedom or funk as improvisational Black studies articulates itself in out-of-the ordinary ways.

However, the institutionalization of Black studies demonstrates the problematic of what to do with its knowledges inside an institution that has produced, and continues to produce, some of the most violent forms of knowledge and political orientations toward Black life-forms. The elevation of Black studies to a method, a way of reading, thinking, and organizing knowledge, outside of a politics of post-Enlightenment modernist destruction can now proceed in violent form and practice to engage blackness without blackness and Black people. The only legitimate Black studies without Black people would have to be a John Brown Black studies. To put it vulgarly, such a Black studies without enslaved people and blackness would mean that white people would have to interrupt the police or any other authority before those authorities enter Black communities or violate Black people. Anything short of that would just be engaged in producing the sensation of freedom, profoundly violating the sovereignty of Black life-forms and their knowledges. A Black studies without Black people is an *after*–Black studies moment, a textual Black figure gazed upon but not heard. Such a Black studies significantly curtails the radical destructive project of Black studies and its potential future politics. In short, a "white Black studies," not a John Brown Black studies, merely banally recuperates the polluted racist contours of the post-Enlightenment modernist project of freedom as white Euro-American intellectual territory.

Significantly, such circumstances can already be glimpsed in places such as Canada, where the formal absence, until recently, of Black studies means that it is smuggled into the institution of the university and lives a fugitive life there. The almost total absence of Black studies in the Canadian academy is probably the clearest way that Canada refuses to acknowledge and, indeed, engage its own anti-Black foundations. In Canadian institutions, actual Black people are made to disappear and only appear as examples of the benevolent nation-state or as nodes in global neoliberal schemes that are meant to further cement the post-Enlightenment modernist project as legitimate and just. The accomplishment is most often achieved through the discourse of rights, which are offered to the formerly subjected, excluded, and killable. What I am remarking on here is the lie of modern life as a postemancipation life.

So, let us here name the recent and ongoing cost of overstepping the limits of the long emancipation for which Black studies must make an accounting: Stephen Lawrence. Wade Lawson. Mark Daly. Trayvon Martin. Jordan Davis. Jonathan Ferrell. Ramarley Graham. Renisha McBride. Jermaine Carby. Eric Garner. Sandra Bland. Andrew Loku. Abdirahman Abdi. And so on and so on. The names exceed these pages.

The problem of emancipation is central to the conditions of Black life. I wanted to call our repeated attention to the substantive difference between the legislative nature of emancipation and the problem of a freedom that is yet to come. I have argued that postemancipation acts of Black life have been consistently interdicted, thereby preempting and often violently preventing Black life from authorizing its own desires for bodily autonomy. Stuck in the process of fully breaking from the logics of slavery and plantation economy, Black people have found ourselves in the long emancipation. The phrase *the long emancipation* does not simply suggest that Black people are still enslaved, but rather it insists that Black people continually are prohibited and interdicted from authorizing what exactly freedom might look like and mean for them collectively. Indeed, such conditions mean that asserting a notion of freedom for Black people, one routed in the critique of capital, remains barely possible. The barely possible exists because the measures of life remain deeply rooted in capital and its subsidiaries, so to refuse capital is to refuse a sort of life. Thus, making millions as movie and television celebrities, sports players, formal politicians, and businesspeople is the measure of Black success and taken as substantive change meant to signal that an anti-Black system is in transition. And yet this is not to say that Black people might not engage in acts of what we might cautiously call agency or what I have called funk. As Saidiya Hartman has noted in the US context concerning emancipation: "The vision of former masters and former slaves as equal members of the national community incited a wave of reaction registered in the opposition to the Thirteenth Amendment, the imposition of the Black Codes, and the pervasiveness of racist terror."[1] The Anglo-Caribbean preceded the United States, and the Lusophone and Spanish Caribbean followed with similar interdictions marking the limits of juridical and legislative emancipation all with practices meant to interdict Black agency or acts of practice or what we might call Black freedom, resulting in the long and ongoing emancipation.

We might argue that contemporary Black "feminist" scholars have asked us to notice the structure, infrastructure, and architecture of racism and specifically antiblackness in deeply profound ways. Despite many Black feminists' difficult relationship with a particular narrative of feminism, their work has pointed us in a direction that requires new feminist readings of the archive. Christina Sharpe and Simone Browne have (re)turned our thinking to the logics of the ship and its pervasive expansion into our present-future. Katherine McKittrick and Jemima Pierre have asked us to attend to the work of colonization in the Americas and Africa as logics of both plantation economy and thought and colonization as the production of the "native-other" in Africa and thus the production of race, which continues to haunt the ways in which Black peoples are apprehended in the world. What their insights and, quite frankly, their ransacking of the archive of thought do for me and for us is to allow a putting together of the historical and the contemporary in a discontinuous fashion that sheds light on the now of Black experience and life. I find it interesting, for example, that in their work they have all resisted the return to marronage and fugitivity. Those two terms resuscitated through the work of Fred Moten and Neil Roberts have been extended to mean a kind of freedom.[2] Indeed, Black women scholars in their contributions seem to be cautious about the ways in which the "big" narratives of freedom might thwart our understanding of what is at stake. Their own articulations, small by no means, have instead asked us to read differently. I want to suggest that their approach is one we might want to more vigorously embrace vis-à-vis the "big" narrative of freedom's moves.

Recent debates in political theory having turned to *fugitivity* and *marronage* as terms both to highlight Black unfreedom and to mark Black renegade flights of desire for freedom as actual freedom remain limited conceptions of freedom for me. I take a different position. The turn to terms like *fugitivity* and *marronage*, with their slim historical references in historical claims, belies or rather highlights the limits of emancipation as freedom and liberation. Concurrently, our turn to these terms demonstrates exhaustion with how unfreedom still frames Black livability and Black life. It is in part my argument that emancipation, fugitivity, and marronage are limited frames for thinking Black freedom beyond their empirical indexes. By this I mean that each term, even when accompanied by action, only makes sense in the space of unfreedom and thus cannot be constituted as freedom. These terms mark the interstices of Black desires for freedom. To hold them as radical Black forms of freedom is to deny that each term and its practice is dependent on unfreedom being present, and indeed each term only makes sense and can only be felt in a full condition of unfreedom. What I mean is that fugitivity and marronage only come to us as the outcome of an encirclement of unfreedom. Indeed, Black unfreedom and anti-Black violence are a priori to fugitivity and marronage, and once we acknowledge this concern, the question of how to think freedom takes on a different tenor.

Similarly, the turn to marronage and maroons encircled by freedom's violence is not an adequate frame for thinking post-Enlightenment Black desires for freedom. Flight is not freedom and neither is subterfuge. Marronage is a temporal self-emancipation that must collude with its other — captivity. Making the claim that I am making is not to undo what maroon communities have meant historically; rather, I want to draw our attention to the limits of recuperating such strategies for our now. In fact, I would argue that if the plantation is a proto-state, we need to think carefully about the détente between maroon communities and the plantation apparatus as a moment that prohibits the potential for Black freedom rather than a moment that provides us a lens onto or into freedom. In short, we need to be more critical of Nanny and Quilumbo, and refuse the romance story that they are quickly becoming in some forms of political theory. Furthermore, it might be necessary that each time marronage and fugitivity are invoked, Haiti's revolution stands beside them as the potential and limit case of freedom and unfreedom. Significantly, then, my argument is premised on the claim that fugitivity and marronage are freedom's violence. To recast these important strategies of resistance as freedom's violence is to highlight that we still live in an era awaiting a "freedom yet to come."

The indignities that Black beings have suffered and continue to suffer, whether in the bellies of slave ships, the corridors of airports and schools, or the rafts of Lampedusa, demand a new perspective. The social site of these indignities is the accreted accumulation of knowledges designed and launched against Black being. Browne's return to the archive of transatlantic slavery as the foundation of the thought of surveillance is a nuanced yet radical gesture for a better conversation that moves us closer to a new perspective. A different political perspective, one grounded in acknowledging the limits of fugitive life and maroon community, alerts us to the ways in which marronage and fugitivity as strategies and furthermore forms of "freedom" remain limited and incomplete modes of a thwarted radical imaginary and political transformation in our time.

I turned to Simone Browne as a way to make clear how the proto-plantation – cum – state and the modern state retain and are the harbinger of unfreedom. To make such a claim is to repeat, we are not free, but we are not free in different ways. For Black peoples unfreedom is the sine qua non of our very being given our invention as the outcome of transatlantic slavery. Take, for example, the Trelawney Town, Jamaica, maroons' "deportation" to Nova Scotia in 1796. This "deportation" opens up the question of what exactly was maroon freedom? How did maroons protect their "freedom" encircled by the unfreedom of the slaveholding plantation proto-state? A more useful question for me is, how does thinking with marronage open up new ways to notice the multiple forms of different unfreedoms in the face of an illusive freedom?

Following Hartman's work, we might understand that the ground from which Black life proceeds is still one of emancipation. We are still in the administrative jurisdiction of emancipation. But, like Nina Simone, we know what freedom is, and in the performance (of refusal, in the taking hold of our bodies, making, etc.), we might experience the dangerous feeling of freedom, that overstepping of emancipation's confinement.

Here I return us to saggin' pants and their ethics as an example I have continually used because it enfolds all the problems of capital, Black bodily autonomy, and the multiple ways in which the state intervenes to interdict small acts of Black freedom or even the assertion of its possibility. City ordinances banning saggin' pants point to the ways in which acts of practice that suggest bodily autonomy and thus a potential Black freedom are interdicted in an attempt to curtail such acts of freedom. The Black Codes, vagrancy laws, and notions of Black idleness are all historically related to these contemporary saggin' pants and previous baseball cap – wearing ordinances. Black people's volition and will to attain some measure of control over our bodies are an affront to a deeply ingrained logic in which Black people are not supposed to own our bodies. Because saggin' pants resist a certain kind of capitalization, they are often outlawed. In this work, I argue that a saggin' pants ethics and a funk ethics then is an attempt to keep alive forms of Black resistance and acts of practice that animate Black life beyond capital, not just in opposition to it. These acts of practice in which Black people attempt to self-authorize their own modes of being in the world are always at some point violently apprehended. Nonetheless, such an ethics, as I insist on calling it, announces to a capitalist world, "I know you mean me no good," and it forces a confrontation with all the forces arrayed against Black personhood as I have stated previously in this work. All those forces that seek to take even the meager elements of the sustenance of life away from us and, even still, that seek to take the command of our own bodies from us too, still insisting that racial capital and the laboring commodity remain our fate, even as Black lives now drift into wasted lives in the time of the long emancipation. And yet we as Black people reanimate those same lives intramurally, with acts of practice still awaiting invention. For what is Black life if not constant, unceasing invention in the time of this long emancipation?

1. MOVING TOWARD BLACK FREEDOM

1 Saidiya V. Hartman, *Scenes of Subjection: Terror, Slavery, and Self-Making in Nineteenth-Century America* (New York: Oxford University Press, 1997), 31.

2 Wilderson writes, "White people are, ipso facto, deputized in the face of Black people, whether they know it (consciously) or not." Frank B. Wilderson, *Red, White and Black: Cinema and the Structure of U.S. Antagonisms* (Durham, NC: Duke University Press, 2010), 82.

3 I am referring here to the practice of apprenticeship in the United States and the Caribbean. Also at play here are prison convict work camps and vagrancy and morality laws and clauses.

4 Toni Morrison, *Beloved* (New York: Plume Books, 1988), 88–89.

5 Robin D. G. Kelley, "Looking to Get Paid: How Some Black Youth Put Culture to Work," in *Yo' Mama's Disfunktional! Fighting the Culture Wars in Urban America* (Boston: Beacon Press, 1997), 43–77.

6 The Kardashians are an example of how white women remake parts of their bodies to accentuate them. The very body parts considered ugly or unattractive on Black women's bodies are now deemed beautiful in their "artificial" enhancements on white women's bodies — lips and buttocks being the most popular.

7 Frantz Fanon, *Black Skin, White Masks*, trans. Charles Lam Markmann (New York: Grove Books, 1967); Sylvia Wynter, "1492: A New World View," in *Race, Discourse, and the Origin of the Americas: A New World View*, ed. Vera Lawrence Hyatt and Rex Nettleford (Washington, DC: Smithsonian Institution Press, 1995), 1–57.

3. DEATH AND FREEDOM

1 Richard Iton, *In Search of the Black Fantastic: Politics and Popular Culture in the Post–Civil Rights Era* (New York: Oxford University Press, 2008). See in particular the chapter "Round Trips on the Black Star Line," 195–258.

2 Dionne Brand, *A Map to the Door of No Return: Notes to Belonging* (Toronto: Doubleday Canada, 2001), 25.

4. BLACK DEATH

1 Sylvia Wynter, "No Humans Involved: An Open Letter to My Colleagues," in *Voices of the Black Diaspora* 8, no. 2 (Fall 1992): 12–16 (excerpt); and in *Forum N.H.I: Knowledge for the 21st Century* 1, no. 1 (Fall 1994): 42–73 (complete document); quotation on 49.

2 Wynter, "No Humans Involved."

3 Wynter, "No Humans Involved," 70.

5. PLANTATION ZONES

1 Katherine McKittrick, "Plantation Futures," *Small Axe* 17, no. 3 (42) (2013): 3.

6. DIASPORA STUDIES

1 I use the term *Black diaspora* as opposed to *African diaspora* or *Afrodiaspora* because for me the impossibility and the complicatedness of any return to an imagined or lost homeland called Africa highlights the ethnodistinctiveness of the latter terms. I understand the instability of the invented, always uncertain marker *Black* as holding many possibilities for reparations within the New World, where blackness in its most potent forms was invented. See Rinaldo Walcott, "Pedagogy and Trauma: The Middle Passage, Slavery, and the Problem of Creolization," in *Between Hope and Despair: The Pedagogical Encounter with Historical Remembrance*, ed. Roger I. Simon, Sharon Rosenberg, and Claudia Eppert (Lanham, MD: Rowman and Littlefield, 2000), 135–52.

2 Bartolomé de Las Casas, *A Short Account of the Destruction of the Indies* (London: Penguin Books, 1992).

3 This is why the debate on reparations in the United States and elsewhere has been such an impoverished one. The inability to think the genocide of Indigenous populations alongside ongoing colonization means that any meaningful debate on reparations for transatlantic slavery proceeds on the terms of European conceptions of the world. And in such a worldview, reparations for those crimes only become thinkable in the aftermath of the Second World War and the Universal Declaration of Human Rights. Thus, any conversation about reparations must take seriously the issues of land, power, and coloniality/colonialism as a central aspect of its purview.

4 In particular I am thinking of the many New World religions and spiritualities that have ushered in numerous cosmologies of the world. These practices, ideas, and beliefs have come out of the brutal encounters of European expansion, but reading them only with a context of brutality would not adequately account for the collective appeal, meaning, and power they hold today.

5 See the now and still important works *Capitalism and Slavery*, by Eric Williams (Chapel Hill: University of North Carolina Press, 1994); *How Europe Underdeveloped Africa*, by Walter Rodney (Washington, DC: Howard University Press, 1982); and, most recently, Saskia Sassen's expansive "historical" document, *Ter-*

ritory. Authority. Rights: From Medieval to Global Assemblages (Princeton, NJ: Princeton University Press, 2008), esp. chap. 3.

6 I am thinking of recent elections in Latin America, Indigenous resistance in North America (most recently Six Nations/Caledonia in what we call Canada), and the immigrant/migrant movement in what we call the United States.

7 Stuart Hall, "Creolization, Diaspora, and Hybridity in the Context of Globalization," in Créolité and Creolization: Documenta11_Platform3, ed. Okwui Enwezor et al. (Kassel, Germany: Hatje Cantz, 2003), 185–98.

8 Walter Mignolo, The Idea of Latin America (Malden, MA: Blackwell, 2005), 153.

9 National independence movements, the US civil rights movement, Indigenous movements, and various kinds of land reclamation movements have all forced revisions of the category of the human, making it more expansive. We also must see feminist and queer movements within a similar light—a resignifying and expanding of the terms of humanhood.

10 For example, see the works of Afua Cooper (The Hanging of Angélique: The Untold Story of Canadian Slavery and the Burning of Old Montreal [Toronto: HarperCollins, 2006]; Peter Linebaugh and Marcus Rediker (The Many-Headed Hydra: Sailors, Slaves, Commoners, and the Hidden History of the Revolutionary Atlantic [Boston: Beacon Press, 2013]); Simon Schama (Rough Crossings: Britain, the Slaves and the American Revolution [Toronto: Viking Canada, 2005]); and Ronald Segal (The Black Diaspora: Five Centuries of the Black Experience outside Africa [New York: Farrar, Straus and Giroux, 1995]).

11 Linebaugh and Rediker, The Many-Headed Hydra.

7. THE ATLANTIC REGION AND 1492

1 Paul Gilroy, The Black Atlantic: Modernity and Double Consciousness (Cambridge, MA: Harvard University Press, 1993).

2 Sibylle Fischer, Modernity Disavowed: Haiti and the Cultures of Slavery in the Age of Revolution (Durham, NC: Duke University Press, 2004), 22.

3 Fischer, Modernity Disavowed, 24.

4 Paul Tiyambe Zeleza, "Rewriting the African Diaspora: Beyond the Black Atlantic," African Affairs 104, no. 414 (2005): 35, 38.

5 Saidiya Hartman, Lose Your Mother: A Journey along the Atlantic Slave Route (New York: Farrar, Straus and Giroux, 2007).

6 I borrow the term racial contract from Charles Mills.

7 Again, it is crucial to keep in mind the ways in which various New World religions call on "Africa," but also the ways in which various New World protest movements have made use of Africa as mostly a concern about here. Thus, Africa means and comes into play meaning many different things, some of which are in accord with the continent itself but much of which is not. Both Rastafarianism and Back to Africa movements are examples of this dynamic.

8 See Jamaica Kincaid, "Flowers of Empire," Harper's, April 1996.

9 Toni Morrison, "Home," in *The House That Race Built: Black Americans, U.S. Terrain*, ed. Wahneema Lubiano (New York: Pantheon Books, 1997), 3–13.

10 I am thinking here of the existence of the Kriolles in Sierra Leone, of Liberia; and movements/religions like Rastafari.

11 Derek Walcott, "A Far Cry from Africa," in *Collected Poems 1948–1984* (New York: Farrar, Straus and Giroux, 1986), 17.

12 Derek Walcott, "The Schooner Flight, " in *Collected Poems 1948–1984*, 345–61.

8. NEW STATES OF BEING

1 Houston A. Baker Jr., *Modernism and the Harlem Renaissance* (Chicago: University of Chicago Press, 2013), 15.

9. THE LONG EMANCIPATION

1 Here I am thinking of fortress Europe, in particular, violent attacks across Europe in places like Germany, France, and Italy on African migrants; and in North America Canada, the United States, and Mexico all either enforcing to the letter or making changes to migration policies to inhibit and even make illegal Black people crossing their borders, especially Haitians.

2 Sylvia Wynter, "Columbus, the Ocean Blue," in *Poetics of the Americas: Race, Founding, and Textuality*, ed. Bainard Cowan and Jefferson Humphries (Baton Rouge: Louisiana State University Press, 1997), 153.

3 Rodney, *How Europe Underdeveloped Africa*.

4 Wynter, "Columbus, the Ocean Blue," 159.

5 Wynter, "Columbus, the Ocean Blue," 159.

6 Jemima Pierre, *The Predicament of Blackness: Postcolonial Ghana and the Politics of Race* (Chicago: University of Chicago Press, 2012), 19.

7 Hall, "Creolization, Diaspora, and Hybridity in the Context of Globalization," 195.

8 Hall, "Creolization, Diaspora, and Hybridity in the Context of Globalization," 196.

9 Hall, "Creolization, Diaspora, and Hybridity in the Context of Globalization," 295.

10 Hall, "Creolization, Diaspora, and Hybridity in the Context of Globalization," 196.

10. CATASTROPHE, WAKE, HAUNTOLOGY

1 Wynter, "Columbus, the Ocean Blue," 153.

2 Wynter, "Columbus, the Ocean Blue," 147.

3 Wilderson, *Red, White and Black*, 18.

4 Christina Sharpe, *In the Wake: On Blackness and Being* (Durham, NC: Duke University Press, 2016), 33.

5 Jacques Derrida, *Specters of Marx: The State of the Debt, the Work of Mourning, and the New International*, trans. Peggy Kamuf (New York: Routledge, 1994), xviii.

6 Derrida, *Specters of Marx*, xix.

7 Derrida, *Specters of Marx*, 37.

11. BODIES OF WATER

1 See Édouard Glissant, *Poetics of Relation*, trans. Betsy Wing (Ann Arbor: University of Michigan Press, 1997), 138.

12. SLAVE SHIP LOGICS/LOGISTICS

1 United Nations Human Rights Office of the High Commissioner, *Situation of Migrants in Transit* (Geneva: Office of the High Commissioner for Human Rights, 2016), www.ohchr.org/Documents/Issues/Migration/StudyMigrants/ OHCHR_2016_Report-migrants-transit_EN.pdf.

2 Simone Browne, "Everybody's Got a Little Light under the Sun: Black Luminosity and the Visual Culture of Surveillance," *Cultural Studies* 26, no. 4 (2012): 542; and in Simone Browne, *Dark Matters: On the Surveillance of Blackness* (Durham, NC: Duke University Press, 2015), 63–88.

3 See Browne, *Dark Matters*; Martha Jones, *Birthright Citizens: A History of Race and Rights in Antebellum America* (Cambridge: Cambridge University Press, 2018); Alondra Nelson, *The Social Life of DNA: Race, Reparations, and Reconciliation after the Genome* (Boston: Beacon Press, 2016).

13. PROBLEM OF THE HUMAN, OR THE VOID OF RELATIONALITY

1 Sylvia Wynter, "Unsettling the Coloniality of Being/Power/Truth/Freedom: Towards the Human, after Man, Its Overrepresentation—an Argument," *CR: The New Centennial Review* 3, no. 3 (2003): 257–337.

2 Wilderson, *Red, White and Black*, 18.

3 Wynter, "Unsettling the Coloniality of Being/Power/Truth/Freedom."

14. NO HAPPY STORY

1 Sylvia Wynter, "On Disenchanting Discourse: 'Minority' Literary Criticism and Beyond," in *The Nature and Context of Minority Discourse*, ed. Abdul R. Jan-Mohamed and David Lloyd (New York: Oxford University Press, 1990), 449.

2 See Ruth Wilson Gilmore, *Golden Gulag: Surplus, Crisis, and Opposition in Globalizing California* (Berkeley: University of California Press, 2007).

3 Bonita Lawrence and Enakshi Dua, "Decolonizing Anti-racism," *Social Justice* 32, no. 4 (2005): 120–43; Zainab Amadahy and Bonita Lawrence, "Indigenous Peoples and Black People in Canada: Settlers or Allies?," in *Breaching the Colonial Contract: Anti-colonialism in the US and Canada*, ed. A. Kempf (Dordrecht, Netherlands: Springer, 2009), 105–36.

4 Jared Sexton, "People-of-Color-Blindness: Note on the Afterlife of Slavery," *Social Text* 28, no. 2 (103) (2010): 31–56.

5 Amadahy and Lawrence, "Indigenous Peoples and Black People in Canada."

6 Peter James Hudson, "Imperial Designs: The Royal Bank of Canada in the Caribbean," *Race and Class: A Journal on Racism, Empire and Globalization* 52, no. 1 (2010): 33–48. For a further development, see also Peter James Hudson, *Bankers and Empire: How Wall Street Colonized the Caribbean* (Chicago: University of Chicago Press, 2017).

7 Lindon Barrett, *Blackness and Value: Seeing Double* (Cambridge: Cambridge University Press, 1999).

8 Lawrence and Dua, "Decolonizing Anti-racism"; Amadahy and Lawrence, "Indigenous Peoples and Black People in Canada."

9 Amadahy and Lawrence, "Indigenous Peoples and Black People in Canada," 127.

10 Wynter, "1492"; Wilderson, *Red, White and Black*.

15. I REALLY WANT TO HOPE

1 Attawapiskat has emerged as a site of contention in Canada settler colonial debates because of the poverty, suicides, and other social maladies that affect this remote community. In 2013 the chief of Attawapiskat, Theresa Spence, went on a hunger strike for forty-three days in Ottawa to highlight what can only be described as the brutal evidence of ongoing colonialism.

2 Frantz Fanon, *The Wretched of the Earth*, trans. Constance Farrington (New York: Grove Press, 1963).

3 Rinaldo Walcott, "Disgraceful: Intellectual Dishonesty, White Anxieties, and Multicultural Critique Thirty-Six Years Later," in *Home and Native Land: Unsettling Multiculturalism in Canada*, ed. May Chazan et al. (Toronto: Between the Lines, 2011), 15–30.

4 Edward Kamau Brathwaite, *Middle Passages: A Lecture*, audio CD (Toronto: Sandberry Press, 2006).

16. FUNK: A BLACK NOTE ON THE HUMAN

1 Iton, *In Search of the Black Fantastic*, 15.

17. NEWNESS

1 Wynter, "1492."

2 Toni Morrison, *The Bluest Eye* (New York: Vintage International, 2007), 86.

3 Derrick May in John Akomfrah's cinematic essay *Last Angel of History* (Brooklyn, NY: Icarus Films, 1997).

4 Kenneth Warren, *What Was African American Literature?* (Cambridge, MA: Harvard University Press, 2011); Nicholas Payton, "Black American Music and the Jazz Tradition," April 30, 2014, https://nicholaspayton.wordpress.com/2014/04/30/black-american-music-and-the-jazz-tradition/.

5 Hannah Arendt, *Essays in Understanding, 1930–1954: Formation, Exile, and Total-itarianism* (New York: Schocken Books, 1994), 131.

18. TOWARD A SAGGIN' PANTS ETHICS

1 LaMonda Horton-Stallings, *Mutha' Is Half a Word: Intersections of Folklore, Vernacular, Myth, and Queerness in Black Female Culture* (Columbus: Ohio State University Press, 2007), 6.
2 Scott Poulson-Bryant, *Hung: A Meditation on the Measure of Black Men in America* (New York: Doubleday, 2005), 7.
3 Rinaldo Walcott, "Keeping the Black Phallus Erect: Gender and the Construction of Black Masculinity in *Boyz n the Hood*," *CineAction*, no. 30 (Winter 1992): 68–74.
4 David Marriott, *On Black Men* (Edinburgh: Edinburgh University Press, 2000), xiv.
5 Marriott, *On Black Men*, xiv.

19. BLACK MEN, STYLE, AND FASHION

1 A sample of saggin' pants ordinances: Town Council Dalcambre, Louisiana, 2007; Opa-lock, Florida, 2010; Town Council Wildwood, New Jersey, 2013; Timmonsville, South Carolina, 2016.
2 Angela McRobbie, *In the Culture Society: Art, Fashion and Popular Music* (Oxford: Routledge, 1999), 144.
3 Richard Sennett, *The Culture of the New Capitalism* (New Haven, CT: Yale University Press, 2007), 178.
4 Sennett, *The Culture of the New Capitalism*, 181.
5 Saidiya Hartman, "The Terrible Beauty of the Slum," *Brick*, no. 99 (July 2017), https://brickmag.com/the-terrible-beauty-of-the-slum/.
6 McRobbie, *In the Culture Society*, 106.
7 Sennett, *The Culture of the New Capitalism*, 86.
8 Rinaldo Walcott, "Reconstructing Manhood; or, The Drag of Black Masculinity," *Small Axe* 13, no. 1 (2009): 75–89.

20. NO FUTURE

1 Dr. Monteiro charged that his contract at Temple University was not renewed because of the nature of the political work he was doing as a Black studies professor in the classroom and beyond. In particular, Dr. Monteiro's teaching and activism had a focus on Temple University and its impact on the surrounding Black communities, making his firing appear complicit with the university's attempt to interrupt his work against its practices.
2 Lawrence Hill, *Dear Sir, I Intend to Burn Your Book: An Anatomy of a Book Burning* (Edmonton: University of Alberta Press and Canadian Literature Centre, 2013), 4–5.
3 On the reference to Rihanna, see Jamilah King, "Dutch Magazine Apologizes for

Calling Rihanna a 'Niggabitch,'" *ColorLines*, December 20, 2011, https://www
.colorlines.com/articles/dutch-magazine-apologizes-calling-rihanna-niggabitch.
The controversy that ensued at fashion magazine *Jackie* led to the resignation of
its editor.

4 Lupe Fiasco, "Around My Way (Freedom Ain't Free)," from *Food & Liquor II: The
Great American Rap* (New York: Atlantic Records, 2012).

21. (FUTURE) BLACK STUDIES

1 Sabine Broeck, "Never Shall We Be Slaves: Locke's *Treatises*, Slavery, and Early
European Modernity," in *Blackening Europe: The African American Presence*, ed.
Heike Raphael-Hernandez (New York: Routledge, 2003), 239.

2 Dylan Rodriguez, "Inhabiting the Impasse: Racial/Racial-Colonial Power, Genocide Poetics, and the Logic of Evisceration," *Social Text* 33, no. 3 (124) (2015):
19–44.

3 Dionne Brand, *The Blue Clerk: Ars Poetica in 59 Verses* (Toronto: McClelland and
Stewart/Penguin Random House Canada Limited, 2018), 166–68.

22. THE LONG EMANCIPATION REVISITED

1 Hartman, *Scenes of Subjection*, 185.

2 Fred Moten, *In the Break: The Aesthetics of the Black Radical Tradition* (Durham,
NC: Duke University Press, 2003); Neil Roberts, *Freedom as Marronage* (Chicago: University of Chicago Press, 2015).

Akomfrah, John, dir. *Last Angel of History*. Brooklyn, NY: Icarus Films, 1997.

Amadahy, Zainab, and Bonita Lawrence. "Indigenous Peoples and Black People in Canada: Settlers or Allies?" In *Breaching the Colonial Contract: Anti-colonialism in the US and Canada*, edited by A. Kempf, 105–36. Dordrecht, Netherlands: Springer, 2009.

Arendt, Hannah. *Essays in Understanding, 1930–1954: Formation, Exile, and Totalitarianism*. New York: Schocken Books, 1994.

Baker, Houston A., Jr. *Modernism and the Harlem Renaissance*. Chicago: University of Chicago Press, 2013.

Barrett, Lindon. *Blackness and Value: Seeing Double*. Cambridge: Cambridge University Press, 1999.

Bauman, Zygmunt. *Wasted Lives: Modernity and Its Outcasts*. Oxford: Polity, 2004.

Brand, Dionne. *The Blue Clerk: Ars Poetica in 59 Verses*. Toronto: McClelland and Stewart/Penguin Random House Canada Limited, 2018.

Brand, Dionne. *A Map to the Door of No Return: Notes to Belonging*. Toronto: Doubleday Canada, 2001.

Brathwaite, Edward Kamau. *Middle Passages: A Lecture*. Audio CD. Toronto: Sandberry Press, 2006.

Broeck, Sabine. "Never Shall We Be Slaves: Locke's *Treatises*, Slavery, and Early European Modernity." In *Blackening Europe: The African American Presence*, edited by Heike Raphael-Hernandez, 235–47. New York: Routledge, 2003.

Browne, Simone. *Dark Matters: On the Surveillance of Blackness*. Durham, NC: Duke University Press, 2015.

Browne, Simone. "Everybody's Got a Little Light under the Sun: Black Luminosity and the Visual Culture of Surveillance." *Cultural Studies* 26, no. 4 (2012): 542–64.

Byrd, Jodi. *The Transit of Empire: Indigenous Critiques of Colonialism*. Minneapolis: University of Minnesota Press, 2011.

Cooper, Afua. *The Hanging of Angélique: The Untold Story of Canadian Slavery and the Burning of Old Montreal*. Toronto: HarperCollins, 2006.

Derrida, Jacques. *Specters of Marx: The State of the Debt, the Work of Mourning, and the New International*. Translated by Peggy Kamuf. New York: Routledge, 1994.

Derrida, Jacques, and Anne Dufourmantelle. *Of Hospitality*. Translated by Rachel Bowlby. Stanford, CA: Stanford University Press, 2000.

Fanon, Frantz. *Black Skin, White Masks*. Translated by Charles Lam Markmann. New York: Grove Press, 1967.

Fanon, Frantz. *The Wretched of the Earth*. Translated by Constance Farrington. New York: Grove Press, 1963.

Fiasco, Lupe. "Around My Way (Freedom Ain't Free)." From *Food & Liquor II: The Great American Rap*. New York: Atlantic Records, 2012.

Fischer, Sibylle. *Modernity Disavowed: Haiti and the Cultures of Slavery in the Age of Revolution*. Durham, NC: Duke University Press, 2004.

Garbus, Liz, dir. *What Happened, Miss Simone?* Los Gatos, CA: Netflix, 2015.

Gilmore, Ruth Wilson. *Golden Gulag: Surplus, Crisis, and Opposition in Globalizing California*. Berkeley: University of California Press, 2007.

Gilroy, Paul. *The Black Atlantic: Modernity and Double-Consciousness*. Cambridge, MA: Harvard University Press, 1995.

Glissant, Édouard. *Poetics of Relation*. Translated by Betsy Wing. Ann Arbor: University of Michigan Press, 1997.

Hall, Stuart. "Creolization, Diaspora, and Hybridity in the Context of Globalization." In *Créolité and Creolization: Documenta11_Platform3*, edited by Okwui Enwezor, Carlos Basualdo, Ute Meta Bauer, Susanne Ghez, Sarat Maharaj, Mark Nash, and Octavio Zaya, 185–98. Kassel, Germany: Hatje Cantz, 2003.

Hartman, Saidiya. *Lose Your Mother: A Journey along the Atlantic Slave Route*. New York: Farrar, Straus and Giroux, 2007.

Hartman, Saidiya. *Scenes of Subjection: Terror, Slavery, and Self-Making in Nineteenth-Century America*. New York: Oxford University Press, 1997.

Hartman, Saidiya. "The Terrible Beauty of the Slum." *Brick*, no. 99 (July 2017). https://brickmag.com/the-terrible-beauty-of-the-slum/.

Hill, Lawrence. *The Book of Negroes*. Toronto: HarperCollins, 2007.

Hill, Lawrence. *Dear Sir, I Intend to Burn Your Book: An Anatomy of a Book Burning*. Edmonton: University of Alberta Press and Canadian Literature Centre, 2013.

Horton-Stallings, LaMonda. *Mutha' Is Half a Word: Intersections of Folklore, Vernacular, Myth, and Queerness in Black Female Culture*. Columbus: Ohio State University Press, 2007.

Hudson, Peter James. *Bankers and Empire: How Wall Street Colonized the Caribbean*. Chicago: University of Chicago Press, 2017.

Hudson, Peter James. "Imperial Designs: The Royal Bank of Canada in the Caribbean." *Race and Class: A Journal on Racism, Empire and Globalization* 52, no. 1 (2010): 33–48.

Iton, Richard. *In Search of the Black Fantastic: Politics and Popular Culture in the Post–Civil Rights Era*. New York: Oxford University Press, 2008.

James, C. L. R. *Beyond a Boundary*. 1963. Durham, NC: Duke University Press, 1993.

Jones, Martha. *Birthright Citizens: A History of Race and Rights in Antebellum America*. Cambridge: Cambridge University Press, 2018.

Kelley, Robin D. G. *Yo' Mama's Disfunktional! Fighting the Culture Wars in Urban America*. Boston: Beacon Press, 1997.

Kincaid, Jamaica. "Flowers of Empire." *Harper's*, April 1996.

Las Casas, Bartolomé de. *A Short Account of the Destruction of the Indies*. London: Penguin Books, 1992.

Lawrence, Bonita, and Enakshi Dua. "Decolonizing Anti-racism." *Social Justice* 32, no. 4 (2005): 120–43.

Linebaugh, Peter, and Marcus Rediker. *The Many-Headed Hydra: Sailors, Slaves, Commoners, and the Hidden History of the Revolutionary Atlantic.* Boston: Beacon Press, 2013.

Marley, Bob. "Exodus." From *Exodus.* London: Island Records, 1977.

Marley, Bob. "Redemption Song." From *Uprising.* London: Island Records, 1980.

Marriott, David. *On Black Men.* Edinburgh: Edinburgh University Press, 2000.

McKittrick, Katherine. "Plantation Futures." *Small Axe* 17, no. 3 (42) (2013): 1–15.

McRobbie, Angela. *In the Culture Society: Art, Fashion and Popular Music.* Oxford: Routledge, 1999.

Mignolo, Walter. *The Idea of Latin America.* Malden, MA: Blackwell, 2005.

Morrison, Toni. *Beloved.* New York: Plume Books, 1988.

Morrison, Toni. *The Bluest Eye.* New York: Vintage International, 2007.

Morrison, Toni. "Home." In *The House That Race Built: Black Americans, U.S. Terrain,* edited by Wahneema Lubiano, 3–13. New York: Pantheon Books, 1997.

Moten Fred. *In the Break: The Aesthetics of the Black Radical Tradition.* Durham, NC: Duke University Press, 2003.

Nelson, Alondra. *The Social Life of DNA: Race, Reparations, and Reconciliation after the Genome.* Boston: Beacon Press, 2016.

Payton, Nicholas. "Black American Music and the Jazz Tradition." April 30, 2014. https://nicholaspayton.wordpress.com/2014/04/30/black-american-music-and -the-jazz-tradition/.

Pierre, Jemima. *The Predicament of Blackness: Postcolonial Ghana and the Politics of Race.* Chicago: University of Chicago Press, 2012.

Poulson-Bryant, Scott. *Hung: A Meditation on the Measure of Black Men in America.* New York: Doubleday, 2005.

Roberts, Neil. *Freedom as Marronage.* Chicago: University of Chicago Press, 2015.

Rodney, Walter. *How Europe Underdeveloped Africa.* Washington, DC: Howard University Press, 1982.

Rodriguez, Dylan. "Inhabiting the Impasse: Racial/Racial-Colonial Power, Genocide Poetics, and the Logic of Evisceration." *Social Text* 33, no. 3 (124) (2015): 19–44.

Sassen, Saskia. *Territory. Authority. Rights: From Medieval to Global Assemblages.* Princeton, NJ: Princeton University Press, 2008.

Schama, Simon. *Rough Crossings: Britain, the Slaves and the American Revolution.* Toronto: Viking Canada, 2005.

Scott, David. *Refashioning Futures: Criticism after Postcoloniality.* Princeton, NJ: Princeton University Press, 1999.

Segal, Ronald. *The Black Diaspora: Five Centuries of the Black Experience outside of Africa.* Toronto: HarperCollins Canada, 1995.

Sennett, Richard. *The Culture of the New Capitalism.* New Haven, CT: Yale University Press, 2007.

Sexton, Jared. "People-of-Color-Blindness: Note on the Afterlife of Slavery." *Social Text* 28, no. 2 (103) (2010): 31–56.

Sexton, Jared. "The Social Life of Social Death: On Afro-Pessimism and Black Optimism." *InTensions Journal* 5 (Fall/Winter 2011): 1–47.

Sharma, Nandita, and Cynthia Wright. "Decolonizing Resistance, Challenging Colonial States." *Social Justice* 35, no. 3 (2008): 120–38.

Sharpe, Christina. *In the Wake: On Blackness and Being*. Durham, NC: Duke University Press, 2016.

Snyder, Christina. *Slavery in Indian Country: The Changing Face of Captivity in Early America*. Cambridge, MA: Harvard University Press, 2010.

Tate, Greg. *Flyboy in the Buttermilk*. New York: Touchstone Books, 2015.

United Nations Human Rights Office of the High Commissioner. *Situation of Migrants in Transit*. Geneva: Office of the High Commissioner for Human Rights, 2016. www.ohchr.org/Documents/Issues/Migration/StudyMigrants/OHCHR _2016_Report-migrants-transit_EN.pdf.

Walcott, Derek. *Collected Poems 1948–1984*. New York: Farrar, Straus and Giroux, 1986.

Walcott, Rinaldo. "Disgraceful: Intellectual Dishonesty, White Anxieties, and Multicultural Critique Thirty-Six Years Later." In *Home and Native Land: Unsettling Multiculturalism in Canada*, edited by May Chazan, Lisa Helps, Anna Stanley, and Sonali Thakkar, 15–30. Toronto: Between the Lines, 2011.

Walcott, Rinaldo. "Into the Ranks of Man: Vicious Modernism and the Politics of Reconciliation." In *Cultivating Canada: Reconciliation through the Lens of Cultural Diversity*, edited by Ashok Mathur, Jonathan Dewar, and Mike DeGagne, 341–50. Ottawa: Indigenous Healing Foundation, 2011.

Walcott, Rinaldo. "Keeping the Black Phallus Erect: Gender and the Construction of Black Masculinity in *Boyz n the Hood*." *CineAction*, no. 30 (Winter 1992): 68–74.

Walcott, Rinaldo. "Pedagogy and Trauma: The Middle Passage, Slavery, and the Problem of Creolization." In *Between Hope and Despair: The Pedagogical Encounter with Historical Remembrance*, edited by Roger I. Simon, Sharon Rosenberg, and Claudia Eppert, 135–51. Lanham, MD: Rowman and Littlefield, 2000.

Walcott, Rinaldo. "Reconstructing Manhood; or, The Drag of Black Masculinity." *Small Axe* 13, no. 1 (2009): 75–89.

Warren, Kenneth. *What Was African American Literature?* Cambridge, MA: Harvard University Press, 2011.

Wilderson, Frank B. *Red, White and Black: Cinema and the Structure of U.S. Antagonisms*. Durham, NC: Duke University Press, 2010.

Williams, Eric. *Capitalism and Slavery*. Chapel Hill: University of North Carolina Press, 1994.

Wynter, Sylvia. "Columbus, the Ocean Blue." In *Poetics of the Americas: Race, Founding, and Textuality*, edited by Bainard Cowan and Jefferson Humphries, 141–64. Baton Rouge: Louisiana State University Press, 1997.

Wynter, Sylvia. "1492: A New World View." In *Race, Discourse, and the Origin of the Americas: A New World View*, edited by Vera Lawrence Hyatt and Rex Nettleford, 1–57. Washington, DC: Smithsonian Institution Press, 1995.

Wynter, Sylvia. "No Humans Involved: An Open Letter to My Colleagues." *Voices of the Black Diaspora* 8, no. 2 (Fall 1992): 12–16 (excerpt). Also in *Forum N.H.I: Knowledge for the 21st Century* 1, no. 1 (Fall 1994): 42–73 (complete document).

Wynter, Sylvia. "On Disenchanting Discourse: 'Minority' Literary Criticism and Beyond." In *The Nature and Context of Minority Discourse*, edited by Abdul R. JanMohamed and David Lloyd, 432–69. New York: Oxford University Press, 1990.

Wynter, Sylvia. "Towards the Sociogenic Principle: Fanon, Identity, the Puzzle of Conscious Experience, and What It Is Like to Be 'Black.'" In *National Identities and Sociopolitical Changes in Latin America*, edited by Mercedes F. Durán-Cogan and Antonio Gómez-Moriana, 30–66. New York: Routledge, 2001.

Wynter, Sylvia. "Unsettling the Coloniality of Being/Power/Truth/Freedom: Towards the Human, after Man, Its Overrepresentation—an Argument." cr: *The New Centennial Review* 3, no. 3 (Fall 2003): 257–337.

Zeleza, Paul Tiyambe. "Rewriting the African Diaspora: Beyond the Black Atlantic." *African Affairs* 104, no. 414 (2005): 35–68.

INDEX

Abdi, Abdirahman, 10
Africa: and Black diaspora, 28–32; Ghana,
    39–40; and the long emancipation, 39;
    meanings of, 113n7; migration, 38–39, 43,
    48; slavery apologies, 31; underdevelop-
    ment, 38, 43
African blackness, 39–40
Afro-Christian religions, 11
Aglukkaq, Leona, 60
Amadahy, Zainab, 63
Americas: death as mode of being, 19; "dis-
    covery" of, 9–10; undoing, need for, 53.
    See also Black death in the Americas; Can-
    ada; Caribbean; United States
antiblackness: in anti-colonization argu-
    ments, 57–58; European global reign, 56;
    global circulation of, 97, 99–100; postslav-
    ery, 74; producing out-of-placeness, 55;
    settler colonialism, 63; style-politics re-
    vealing, 82–83. See also humanness, Black
    exclusion from
appropriations of vernacular cultures, 7
archipelagos of poverty, 62
Arendt, Hannah, 79
art: Black Arts Movement, 6; music, 79, 87,
    89; of Paulo Nazareth, 15–17. See also funk
Atlantic region, 27–30. See also slavery
Atleo, Shawn, 60
Attawapiskat, 59, 65–67, 116n1
autonomy, 33

Baker, Houston A., Jr., 34
behavior-directing signs, 59, 74
Bellegarde, Perry, 60
belonging, place-based, 67
Beloved (Toni Morrison), 4–5
Beyond a Boundary (C. L. R. James), 1, 10

big dick syndrome, 83–84
Black American Music (BAM), 79
Black Arts Movement, 6
Black Atlantic, The (Paul Gilroy), 27–28
Black being: expanding humanness, 66,
    73; modes of, 5–6; self-authorization,
    108–9; voids of relationality, 44, 56–57, 91;
    Wilderson on, 44, 56–57
Black bodies: Canadian, 67; fantasies of,
    83–84; in funk, 71; modes of being, 5–6;
    production of, 52
Black children, 20–21
Black death: centrality to blackness, 20; com-
    plicating value, 19–20; economics of,
    33–34; and freedom, 11–14; Genocide in
    America, 15; halting movement, 36; ver-
    sus non-Black, 11; orienting Black life, 12;
    spectacularization of, 45–46; state actors,
    12; youth, 21; zones of, 15–17, 34, 53
Black death in the Americas: Black life-
    forms, 9–11; plantation logics, 19–20; as
    zone of, 9, 15–17, 53
Black death-life, 78
Black diaspora: overview of, 23; and Africa,
    28–32; versus African diaspora, 112n1; in-
    stitutions, 31–32; politics, 30; return im-
    possibility, 28–30, 32
Black diaspora studies: Atlantic region focus,
    27–30; goals of, 23; humanness, 25, 31–32;
    power of, 29; universities, 28
Black expressivity. See vernacular cultures
Black feminist scholarship, 106
Black freedom: asserting, 105; creativity, 12;
    eruptions, 4, 6–7; futurity, 99; glimpses of,
    2; global reordering, 5; institutional limit-
    ing of, 105; interruptions, 99–100; matura-
    tion narrative refusal, 3; modernity, 2–3;

Black freedom (*continued*)
movement, 14; opposition to capitalism,
65–66; reclaiming of the body, 4–6; vernacular cultures expressing, 6
Black-Indigenous encounters, 61
Black joy, 89
Black knowledges, 75, 101–2
Black life: challenging value, 19–20; as commodity, 58; death orienting, 12; as liability
and profit, 47; nation-states failing, 42;
plantation logics shaping, 50; spectacularization of, 45–46; state protection, 33–34;
submerged culture, 43
Black life-forms: critical capacities of, 74, 91;
decolonization limits, 75; exceeding containment, 46, 48; as global citizens, 52; humanness, 9–10, 55, 72; migration, 38; modernist freedom expulsion, 101; movement,
10; New World Black people, 32, 74–75,
78; versus partial forms of life, 10; states of
being, 34; term meanings, 9
Black luminosity, 51
Black masculinity: anxieties over usefulness,
88; in capitalist cultures, 88; debates over,
87–88; penises, 83–84; public, 87–90;
types of, 84–85. *See also* fashion
Black movement: Black life-forms, 10; death
halting, 36; factors conditioning, 39–40,
50; forces impelling, 48; freedom, 14;
freedom to leave, 48–49; logics of, 47;
postemancipation, 35–37, 48; as reparation, 52; slave ship logics, 52; slave trade,
31; stakes of, 28
Black musics, 79, 87, 89. *See also* funk
blackness: African versus New World, 39–40;
death's centrality to, 20; decolonial projects
engaging with, 56; invention of, 15; and
modernity, 71; refusals, 2; valuations of, 48
Black out-of-placeness: colonial viewpoints
on, 62–63; constraining Black knowledges,
75; and death, 45, 60; migrants, 48; production of, 44, 55, 60–62, 67
Black popular culture, 87, 89
Black Power, 6
Black queer peoples, 89–90
Black respectability, 6–7, 90
Black salability, 47
Black studies, 91–92, 102–3. *See also* Black
diaspora studies

Black transgender peoples, 89–90
Black unfreedom: and death, 11, 13; decolonial projects confronting, 56; emancipation, 1, 106–7; Euro-American philosophy,
71; fashion, 84; and fugitivity, 106–7; funk
expressing, 75; long emancipation, 13–14,
37; and marronage, 106–8; nativism, 61;
reproduction of, 102; vernacular cultures
expressing, 6
Black women, 7, 111n6
Blyden, Edward, 84
bodies. *See* Black bodies
Book of Negroes, The (Lawrence Hill): in Canada, 93–94, 96–97; cover burnings, 92–93,
95; *Dear Sir, I Intend to Burn Your Book*,
92–97; in the Netherlands, 92–93, 95–97;
popularity of, 93, 98; title of, 92–95, 97; in
the United States, 92, 94–95, 97
border crossing, 51
Bowie, David, 79–80
Brand, Dionne, 12, 35, 101–2
Brathwaite, Kamau, 9, 43–45, 68
Brazeau, Patrick, 60
Broeck, Sabine, 100–101
Browne, Simone, 51, 106–7

Canada: anti-Blackness, 38, 103; Attawapiskat,
59, 65–67, 116n1; Black studies, 91, 102–3;
The Book of Negroes reception, 93–94,
96–97; capitalism, 65–66; colonial practices, 61–63; Indigenous peoples, 59–60,
65; labor movement, 41–42; and transatlantic slavery, 96
capitalism, 26, 63, 65–67
carceral states, 60
Caribbean: archipelago of poverty, 62; culture, 43; Haiti, 9, 49, 107; peoples, 30–31
catastrophe, 44–45, 48, 68
Cherokee Nation, 61
childhood, 20–21
children, 20–21
coloniality: of being, 57; contemporary life,
59; dynamics of, 63; humanness, 56–57, 59,
74; ideological frames of, 56; neoliberal,
60–61; out-of-placeness, 62–63. *See also*
settler colonialism
colonization, arguments against, 57–58
corporate multiculturalism, 100
cosmopolitanism, 52

creativity, 5–7, 12–13, 52
Crummell, Alexander, 84

deadly living, 77
Dear Sir, I Intend to Burn Your Book (Lawrence Hill), 92–97
death. *See* Black death
debt, 49
decolonial projects, 55–56, 67–68
decolonization modes, 75
Derrida, Jacques, 5, 9, 45–46, 56
diaspora, 23–24. *See also* Black diaspora
Douglass, Frederick, 84
drapetomania, 52–53
Du Bois, W. E. B., 84

economics of lynching, 33–34
emancipation: British, 1, 99; dependence on
    unfreedom, 106–7; versus freedom, 2,
    36–37, 44, 49, 105; hauntology, 46; intentions of, 99; limits, 3; meanings of, 1–2;
    movement problematics, 35–37; regional
    differences, 37; resistance to, 105; subordinating functions, 4, 111n3. *See also* long
    emancipation
ethnicization, 40
European Enlightenment, 23, 31, 72, 79
European expansion: geopolitics following,
    23–24; global reordering, 25–26; humanness, 9–10; spiritualities resulting from,
    112n4. *See also* slavery

Fanon, Frantz, 7, 9, 39, 57, 69
fashion: appropriations of, 13; and big dick
    syndrome, 84; hip-hop versus gay male, 81;
    as interdiction site, 83; prohibitions, 82, 87;
    style-politics, 81–84; usefulness anxieties,
    88–89. *See also* saggin' pants
feminism, 106
Fiasco, Lupe, 98
Fischer, Sibylle, 27–28
freedom: and death, 11–14; definition of, 1–2;
    versus emancipation, 2, 36–37, 44, 49, 105;
    enslavement as foundation of, 101; and humanness, 55; as imminent, 5; Lockean, 100;
    modernist, 3, 101; of movement, 36; sensations of, 100, 102. *See also* Black freedom
freedom to leave, 48
fugitivity, 106–7
funk: artists, 73, 76–77, 79–80; definitions,
    69, 71; ethics, 77–78, 90, 108; historical

contexts, 75–76; meanings of, 76–77; revolution, 79–80; thinking with, 71, 73

Ghana, 39–40
Gilroy, Paul, 27–28
Glissant, Édouard, 9
globalization, 41, 78
global niggerdom, 97, 100
global reordering, 78–79
Groenberg, Roy, 93, 95–97

Haiti, 9, 49, 107
Haitians, movement of, *41, 43*, 48
Hall, Stuart, 25, 41, 48
Hartman, Saidiya: African production of the
    New World, 28; Black life-forms, 9, 108; on
    emancipation, 105; on fashion, 88; on progressive narratives, 3; the wake, 44–45
hauntology, 44–46, 48–49
Het Negerboek. See Book of Negroes, The
Hill, Lawrence: anticensorship, 93–96; *Dear
    Sir, I Intend to Burn Your Book*, 92–97. See
    also *Book of Negroes, The*
hip-hop culture, 87
Horton-Stallings, LaMonda, 82
Hudson, Peter James, 62
humanism, 7, 45, 57, 71
humanness: Black being expanding, 66, 73;
    Black diaspora studies, 25, 31–32; versus
    Black life-forms, 9; colonial frames, 57;
    definitions of, 71–74; Euro-American expansionism, 9–10; Euro-American narratives of, 73–74; events reshaping, 25, 113n9;
    evolution of, 16–17; as fluctuating, 56; and
    freedom, 55; genres of man, 58; invention
    of, 71–72; management of, 63; production of, 66; resisting, 74; revolution of, 79;
    scholarly embeddedness in, 63
humanness, Black exclusion from: versus
    Black life-forms, 9–10, 55, 72–73; colonial
    legacies, 56, 59; creating Euro-American
    humanity, 34; cultural expression, 12; definition of, 55; drapetomania logics, 52–53;
    Euro-American ideologies, 9; European
    determination of, 57–58; examples of,
    16–17; modern conditions enabling, 72;
    out-of-placeness, 59–60; ships signifying, 49; slavery's legacy, 21; slavery's role
    in, 56, 58
human rights discourses, 10

Indigenous conservatives, 60
Indigenous peoples: arguments against colonization, 57–58; Attawapiskat, 59, 65–67, 116n1; body politic access, 30; capitalism participation, 65; colonization as cultural revolution, 24–25; diaspora studies, 23–24; genocide of, 24, 112n3; justice required, 65; neoliberal alignments, 59
interventions of history, 25, 29
Iton, Richard, 11, 69, 71

James, C. L. R., 1, 10, 33–34
Jamie XX, 79
jazz, 79
joy, 89

Kelley, Robin D. G., 6
Kincaid, Jamaica, 30–31
King, Rodney, 15–16
knowledge as kinship, 28

Lampedusa, Italy, 43, 47, 107
Las Casas, Bartolomé de, 24
Latinx people, 38
Lawrence, Bonita, 63
Linebaugh, Peter, 25
literature of catastrophe, 44, 68
Locke, John, 100
long emancipation, 1, 3, 99, 105; Africa, 39; appropriation, 7; hauntology, 46; language concerns, 97; Middle Passage, 43–44, 48; movement, 44; plantation logics, 50; racial ordering of human life, 74; regional differences, 37; self-ownership, 7; sensations of freedom, 100; unfreedom, 13–14, 37
love songs, 11
lynching, 33–34

Marley, Bob, 1, 35–37, 77
Marriott, David, 81, 84
marronage, 106–8
Martin, Paul, 65
Martin, Trayvon, 13, 97
Martin Family Initiative, 65
maturation narratives, 3
May, Derrick, 77
McKittrick, Katherine, 19–20, 50, 106
McRobbie, Angela, 87–88
medicine, 20
Middle Passage: African underdevelopment, 43; extensions of, 13, 43; invention of

Blackness, 15; long emancipation, 43–44, 48; transformation of bodies, 52
Mignolo, Walter, 25
migration: African, 38–39, 43, 48; Black life-forms, 38; Dionne Brand on, 35; globalization, 41; nation-states, 42; racism structuring, 39; *Situation of Migrants in Transit* report, 51; slave ship logics, 50; violence, 114n1
Mingus, Charles, 78
modernity: Black deformation of, 34; and blackness, 71; freedom under, 3, 101; and funk, 76; heterogeneity of, 27; humanism under, 34; movement, 35; race memory of, 79. *See also* nation-states
Monteiro, Anthony, 91, 117n1
Morrison, Toni, 4–5, 31, 76–77
Moten, Fred, 106
movement: ex-enslaved people, 35–36; freedom of, 36; Haitians, *41*, 43, 48; of labor, 41–42; long emancipation, 44; modernity, 35; slave ship logics, 50. *See also* Black movement; migration

nation-states: ethnocultural identities, 29; failures of, 36, 47; migration fears, 42; myths about, 100; plantation logics, 48, 107–8; refusals of, 32; slavery's legacy, 36; and unfreedom, 107–8
nativism, 61
nativization, 40
Nazareth, Paulo, 15, *16*, *17*
neoliberalism, 59–61, 88–89
Netherlands: anti-Blackness, 96, 117n3; *The Book of Negroes*, 92–93, 95–97; slave trade involvement, 95–96
new humanism, 7, 57
newness, 75
New World Black people, 32, 74–75, 78
no humans involved (NHI), 16
nonhuman life-forms, 74

our studies, 73
out-of-placeness. *See* Black out-of-placeness

Payton, Nicholas, 79
Pierre, Jemima, 39–40, 48, 106
Plantation Futures, 19–20, 50
plantation logics, 48, 50, 52
plantations, 19–20, 48, 107–8
policing: and Black death, 12, 45; and Black

non-humanness, 16–17; prohibiting Black life, 53; vernacular culture, 6
politics of respectability, 90
politics of thought, 67–68
Poulson-Bryant, Scott, 83
publishers, Canadian versus American, 97
pure decolonial projects, 55–56, 67–68

queer peoples, 89–90

race memory, 79
racism. *See* antiblackness; humanness, Black exclusion from
rap, 87, 89
Rediker, Marcus, 25
Reed, Ishmael, 89
remix, 79
reparations, 52, 112n3
respectability, 6–7, 90
Roberts, Neil, 106
Rodney, Walter, 15, 38–40, 43
Rodriguez, Dylan, 101
Rosewood, Florida, 33–34

saggin' pants: and Black ontology, 13; ethics, 81–85, 89–90, 108; example of, *70*; and plantation logics, 52; proscriptions against, 3, *82*, 108; usefulness anxieties, 89
Scott-Heron, Gil, 79, 99
Sennett, Richard, 88–89
sensations of freedom, 100, 102
settler colonialism: antiblackness, 63; contemporary debates, 57; debates on, 60–61; diaspora studies, 23; relational logics, 63; scholarship shortcomings, 61–62; and slavery, 24
Sharpe, Christina, 44–45, 106
ship logics, 50–53, 106–7
ships, 49–50
Simone, Nina, 69, 108
Singleton, John, 33
Situation of Migrants in Transit report, 51
slavery: African state apologies, 31; Canadian involvement in, 96; versus captivity, 56; and contemporary movement, 43; as cultural revolution, 24–25, 112n4; defining Black freedom, 2; denying childhood, 20–21; Dutch involvement in, 95–96; ends of the trade, 47; as haunting, 46; Indigenous perspectives on, 63; invention of Blackness, 15; and Lockean freedom, 100; and settler colonialism, 24. *See also* Middle Passage

slave ship logics, 50–53
Snyder, Christina, 56
species jumps, 77
Spence, Theresa, 116n1
states of being, 34
street corners, 6
style-politics, 81–84
subfunk, 80
submerged culture, 43–44
surveillance, 51–52
survival logics, 52

Tate, Greg, 69
Temple University, 91, 117n1
tidalectics, 43
transatlantic slavery. *See* slavery
transgender peoples, 89–90

unfreedom. *See* Black unfreedom
United States: anti-Black migratory practices, 38; *The Book of Negroes* (Lawrence Hill) in, 92, 94–95, 97; spectacularization of Black death, 46

vernacular cultures, 5–7, 12, 52. *See also* fashion
violence, 33, 59, 114n1
voids of relationality, 44, 56–57, 91

wake, the, 44–45, 48
Walcott, Derek, 32
Warren, Kenneth, 79
white places, 48
white supremacy, 6, 34, 50
white violence, 33
Wilderson, Frank B., III: on deputization of white people, 3, 111n2; on production of Black life-forms, 52; on voids of relationality, 44, 56–57, 91
women, 7, 111n6
Wynter, Silvia: behavior-directing signs, 59; Black death, 15, 19, 53; Black life-forms, 9; Black movement, 40, 48; coloniality of being, 57; on encountering the world, 75; genres of man, 58; on the human, 15–17, 55–56; migration, 38–39; "New World" view, 23; on Otherness, 91; scholarship as political project, 21; on self-expression, 81; transhipped culture, 43; underdeveloped places, 43–44

Zeleza, Paul, 28